MESCHENDORF

Siebenbürger Saxons

I0149952

Meschendorf 12th July 1993

Letter written to cousin Sofie

I am sure you have already been awaiting a letter from me.
As you already know, all siblings, on either sides, nephews
and nieces, have left and are all awaiting letters from me.
Anyway, there is nothing new here. Everything is falling
apart. Church services are only taking place once every
five weeks, with very few people attending. Everything has
become very expensive, and the prices are still rising.
Are you coming home this summer? Your *Hof*(farm yard) looks
abandoned, no human in sight. There is not even any sign
of life on the streets. The wine in the cellar has gone
off and I could not find anyone who wanted to make *Schnaps*
out of it. The weather is constantly changing. Extreme
heat is often followed by a storm, along with torrential
rain and hail. Time is passing, and we are constantly
getting older. My wife is still taking care of her house
duties, the vegetable garden and flowers. I have a lot of
work to do. Raking the ground, mowing the fields, stacking
the hay, and taking care of my bees. Yesterday we were
cleaning the large graveyard removing the weeds that have
been overgrowing the graves. There is no water flowing
through the new water supply. We have not yet come to any
conclusion regarding moving to a home in "Schweischern".
We believe that the best place to be is at our own home.

"So bleibt Altenheim, Altenheim,
wir bleiben in unserem Eigenheim.
Zum Leben haben wir allerhand,
unsere Zukunft liegt in Gotteshand!"¬

"So remains home, home
We stay in our own home.
To live we have a lot of things,
Our future is in Gods hands!"

(Toepfer Friedrich. p. 101 translated by Jessica Klein)

Ahnentafel (genealogical ancestor chart — handwritten, faded)

24	25	26	27	28	29	30	31
geb. 1800	geb. 1803	geb. 1804	geb. 1807	geb. 1814	geb. 1821	geb. 1810	geb. 1815

12	13	14	15
geb. 1827	geb. 1823	geb. 1840	geb. 1841

6	7
... geb. 1855	... geb. 1864

3
... geb. 1891

... geb. 1919.

16	17	18	19	20	21	22	23
geb. 1811	geb. 1814	geb. ?	geb. ?	geb. 1804	geb. 1809	geb. 1807	geb. 1806

8	9	10	11
geb. 1836	geb. 1842	geb. 1831	geb. 1839

4	5
... geb. 1862	... geb. 1861

2
... geb. 1886

1

In Memory of Georg Klein...

CONTENTS

FORWARD   p. 13

INTRODUCTION   p. 15

- Transylvania
- Austrian-Hungarian Empire (Treaty of Trianon)
- German Settlers in Siebenbuergen (Transylvanian Saxons)
- King Geza II
- Goldene Freibrief- Golden Charter
- WWII

MESCHENDORF   p. 33

 -Arrival in Meschendorf
- Property ownership
- Meschendorf Saxon Architecture

     OBERGASSE   p. 61

     ___HOUSE OF MITZ, AGED 101

     - Mitz, last remaining Saxon in Meschendorf
     - Mitz 100th Birthday
     - *Das Stufenalter des Mannes*
     - *Kolchose* during Communism

     ___THE FORTIFIED CHURCH

     - Fortified walls
     - *Speckturm*
     - Church service
     - Role of Church in Saxon community
     - Stolen Church Bells

     ___GERMAN SCHOOL

     - German School
     - Youth Club

CONTENTS

___TANZPLATZ

- *Pfingsten*
- *Kronenfest*
- Weddings
- Christmas

- St Nicholas
- New Years
- Names Day

MITTELGASSE   p. 93

- *Nachbarschaftszeichen*
- Couples Prison
- *Tracht*
- Food

UNTERGASSE   p. 105

___ The Orthodox Romanian Church

- Romanians in Meschendorf
- Reflection of Meschendorf (Helmuth)

CONCLUSION   p. 113

BIBLIOGRAPHY   p. 117

APPENDIX   p. 123

- Interviews

- Drawings

Map of Schafsburger, Hermanstadter, Repster region villages in Transylvania showing Meschendorf in the Central area.

When I was young, I always dreamt of being able to step back in time, to discover a world that I thought was lost. I wished to find the secret portal portrayed in so many stories and myths that would be able to transport me into a different era of time. My grandfather would always tell me about Meschendorf, the Saxon village in Romania where he was born and grew up. The bedtime stories always sounded more like a fairy tale, and a grand exaggeration of how things really were. I could not imagine a village in Europe where people lived in similar conditions as my schoolteacher would describe England hundreds of years ago before the Industrial Revolution. Little did I know that in years to come I would be able to visit Meschendorf, and feel like I have been transported to a time way before I was born. Through this journey I was able to record stories from past residents revealing a culture that survived from the 11th century through to the 19th century almost unchanged, but is now facing extinction. The only things that are remaining are the memories encapsulated within its past Saxon residents, in one of Europe's least known, but most fascinating regions, Transylvania.

"We are in Transylvania; and Transylvania is not England. Our ways are not your ways, and there shall be to you many strange things."
– Bram Stoker, Dracula

The Saxons that settled in Transylvania have no relationship with the Anglo-Saxons, nor the Saxons found in the present German state of Saxony. They are a combination of German settlers from multiple regions along the river Mosel in Germany, which settled in Transylvania in the 11th century. The Transylvanian Saxons origin and nature will be discussed further, although a clear answer to their heritage and 'Saxon' name is unknown.

—— Movement
of German
Settlers to
Transylvania

▒ Meschendorf

INTRODUCTION

In this book I will examine a Saxon village called Meschendorf, located in Transylvania, Romania and the effects mass emigration has had on its landscape, architecture and people. Meschendorf is one of many Saxon villages located in Transylvania that has undergone one of Europe's most dramatic emigration processes within the last 100 years. This resulted in one of the most drastic cultural changes and challenges within Europe. It is fascinating how the German settlers brought with them the German culture from various regions along the Mosel River to create their own preserved community for hundreds of years. Saxon villages were able to sustain their culture, traditions, language, food and dress, in addition to surviving through two world wars and years of communism, yet, today their culture and existence has almost vanished in the time frame of a single generation. How much of a culture is left in a place, and how much of a culture is brought into a place by its inhabitants? Is a place created and transformed depending on the nature of its inhabitants? Or does a place create the people that inhabit it?

Through this book, past cultural customs and changes Meschendorf has undergone through mass emigration will be discussed in the eyes of its past Saxon residents that have now immigrated "back" to Germany, of which my grandfather, Georg Klein, was one.

Georg Klein had lived in Meschendorf the first 19 years of his life; with documents of his family tracing to the 1600's.

The book will explain why the German settlers went to Transylvania followed by a description of the Saxon village. The village will be discussed from its highest point, *Obergasse*, starting with a description of a Saxon home, followed by memories of the last remaining Saxon resident, Martin Werner aged 101, all the way down to the lower part of the village, *Untergasse*, where the newly renovated Orthodox Romanian church is located, a symbol of the changed community. Typical architecture, traditions, festivities, and customs of the Saxons will be discussed in addition to the emotional experiences and changes Meschendorfer Saxons have undergone, mainly within the last century.

THE DISSOLUTION OF AUSTRIA-HUNGARY
The heavy line bounds the old Austro-Hungarian Monarchy. The
light dotted lines show the several provinces. The heavy solid lines
bound the new states formed by the Paris Conference as follows

1. The Republic of Austria
2. The Republic of Hungary
3. The Republic of Czechoslovakia
4. Austrian Territory annexed by Poland
5. Hungarian Territory annexed by Romania
6. The Serbo-Coast-Slovene State (Yugoslavia)
7. Austrian territory annexedy by Italy

On first observation Transylvania gives a picturesque impression. Its landscape comprises of dramatic mountains, and large never ending forests filled with wild animals such as wolves and bears in addition to remains of ancient buildings. Supposedly its people include shepherds, gypsies, and woodcutters, vampires and of course Dracula, a fairy tale come true living within the forests and villages founded by the Saxons in the middle ages. Even Transylvania's literal Latin meaning 'beyond the forest'[1], given by the Hungarians during their occupation for almost a thousand years, shows how Transylvania is almost a make believe, fictitious region. Most people today, who know its existence, would even hesitate where to pinpoint it on the map. For centuries Transylvania has been heavily associated with the existence of Dracula, and vampires -the west have often viewed it as its other or the outsider. Nevertheless once this romantic veil is lifted one notices that the villages are also infested with poor health, poverty and the effects of its communist past.

Transylvania is located in the central part of Romania bounded by the Carpathian Mountains on both the south and east side. The mountains formed a natural border frontier between the East and West, and a boundary between Moldavia and the old principalities of Wallachia, which now with Transylvania makes up modern-Romania.

Throughout history, various empires and peoples dominated Transylvania, such as the Austrian-Hungarian empire (until 1918). It can be described as a 'whirlpool of European races'[2] as various peoples have occupied Transylvania, with some races having great repressions, and others such as the Saxons enjoying unimaginable freedom. In 1918[3], Transylvania became part of Romania through the *'Treaty of Trianon'*, resulting in Romania being a product of multiple incarnations. Romania can be tied to its Slavic neighbours, Greece, Turkey, the former USSR, Hungary and the Saxon Germans; nevertheless most Romanians link their longer past with the Dacians[4].

More than 800 years ago Germans colonized Transylvania on the invitation by the King Geza II of Hungary (1141-1162)[5]. He invited both Germans and Flemish as guests – known as '*Hospites*

---

1   Hannover, Brigitta G. 'Rumaenien entdecken: Kunstschaetze und Naturschoenheiten'. (Berlin. Trescher-Reihe Reisen, 2007).p119
2   Riley, Bronwen. 'Transylvania'. (London. Frances Lincoln Limited, 2007.)p11
3   "Transylvania." Wikipedia, the Free Encyclopedia. 15 Dec. 2011. Web. 3 Dec. 2011. <http://en.wikipedia.org/wiki/Transylvania>.
4   Hannover, Brigitta G. 'Rumaenien entdecken: Kunstschaetze und Naturschoenheiten'. (Berlin. Trescher-Reihe Reisen, 2007).p119
5   ibit

Teutonici et Flandrenses[6]- within the arc of the Carpathians. The Germans mainly settled in *Siebenbürgen* (*Siebenbürger Sachsen*) and later in *Banat* (hence: *Banater Schwaben*). The original role of the German settlers was to cultivate and defend the South-eastern border of the Hungarian Kingdom in addition to protect against the semi nomadic Tartars and Cumans that regularly raided Transylvania between 1241/1242[7]. There are varying historical theories what exactly brought them to emigrate to Transylvania, but the underlying reason was to escape extreme poverty in their homeland Germany. In return German settlers were given free property, attracted by tax incentives along with the guarantee of cultural freedom.

In the mid 12th Century the Saxons settled in Altland or Hermannstadt Province setting up various villages along with seven main towns, which are known as the *Siebenbürgen* (seven boroughs) region. The name *Siebenbürgen* possibly originates from the seven castles the Saxons built, one in each of the seven towns formed. *Siebenbürgen* is also known as *„Das Land hinter den Wäldern*[8] meaning ‚the land behind the woods' due to its rural and often forest landscape. While the majority of Saxons live in rural communities, they also set up towns: some of which gradually grew into sizeable cities.

Siebenbürger Towns

Bistritz – Bistrita
Kronstadt - Brasov
Klausenburg – Cluj-Napoca
Mediasch – Medias
Muehlbach – Sebes
Hermannstadt – Sibiu
Schaessburg - Sighisoara

Although the Saxons are known to hold detailed archives, there is no coherent evidence that locates the Saxons back to a specific region within Germany. In the seventh century there was a strong debate about the origins of the Transylvanian Saxons. Books, such as *„Das Alt- und Neu-teutsche Dacia"*

6   Riley, Bronwen. 'Transylvania'. (London. Frances Lincoln Limited, 2007.) p29
7   Hannover, Brigitta G. 'Rumaenien entdecken: Kunstschaetze und Naturschoenheiten'. (Berlin. Trescher-Reihe Reisen, 2007). 119
8   ibit p.144

Legend of the origin of the Transylvanian Saxons: Pied Piper of Hamelin

(The Old and New German Dacia), published in 1666 by Johannes Troester showed possible links with the Saxons and Dacians, which were strongly linked to German Goths and Thracian Getae[9]. This though, would give the Saxons a predated presence in Transylvania prior to the Hungarians. The idea that Saxons could pre-date the Hungarians, although enjoyed by various Saxons, was slowly dropped by the eighteenth century.

Another legend suggests that the Transylvanian Saxons originated from the children that were lured out of the *Amlasch* (Varghis) cave into Transylvania by the Pied Piper (a Romany) of Hamelin.[10] This story would explain how blue-eyed, fair haired German-speakers that followed ancient customs, lived in Transylvania, although they were far from Germany by thousands of miles.

"In Transylvania there's a tribe,
Of alien people who ascribe
The outlandish ways and dress,
On which their neighbours lay such stress
To their fathers and mothers having risen,
Out of some subterranean prison
Into which they had been trepanned,
Long time ago, in a mighty band,
Out of Hamelin town in Brunswick land,
But how or why they don't understand."
- The Tale of The Pied Piper – Robert Browning

Today there are still debates about the origins of Saxons. It is important not to confuse the name of the Saxons with the present German state of Saxony. The Transylvanian Saxons language and cultural traits in addition to the rules and rituals of the communities, suggests that they come from elsewhere. Many believe that the Saxons originate from the Mosel/Luxembourg region, but it is still not understood how they became known under the name of Saxons in 1204[11]. Others state that they come from parts of Germany, which were historically known

9   Riley, Bronwen. 'Transylvania'. (London. Frances Lincoln Limited, 2007 p 25.
10   Foisel, John. 'Saxons through the Seventeen Centuries: A history of the Transyvanian Saxons'. (Cleveland, Ohio. Central Alliance of Transylvanian Saxons in the United States, 1936.)
11   Ambrosi, Gerhard. "Carl Wolff and the Significance of Co-operative Ideas for the Regional Development of Transylvania." UNIVERSITY OF TRIER, 2002. Web. 3 Dec. 2011. <http://www.siebenbuerger.de/pdf/carl-wolff-ambrosi_englisch.pdf>.

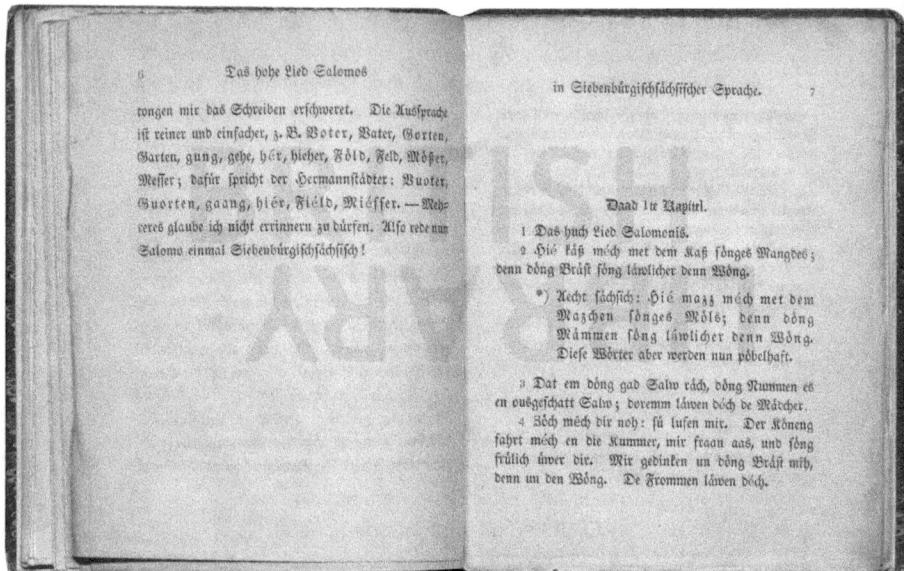

Seivert, J. *Das hohe Lied Salomos in Siebenburgischsachsischer Sprache*

1 Das Lied der Lieder, von Salomo.

2 Er küsse mich mit Küssen seines Mundes, denn deine Liebe ist köstlicher als Wein.

3 An Duft gar köstlich sind deine Salben; ausgegossenes Salböl ist dein Name. Darum lieben dich die Mädchen.

4 Zieh mich dir nach, laß uns eilen! Der König möge mich in seine Gemächer führen! Wir wollen jubeln und uns freuen an dir, wollen deine Liebe preisen mehr als Wein! Mit Recht liebt man dich.

1 The Song of Songs of Solomon.

2 Let him kiss me with kisses of his mouth, for thy love is more delightful than wine.

3 To do delicious fragrance are thy ointments, anointing oil is poured forth thy name. So you love the girl.

4 Draw me after you, let us hurry! Let the king bring me into his chambers! We will rejoice and be glad in you want to praise your love more than wine! By law you love yourself.

as Saxony, and today can be described as being near Liege, Luxembourg and Treves.[12] This would also explain why the Saxon dialect could be compared to that of past Luxembourg, which is difficult for a modern German to understand.

When my Grandfather visited Luxemburg, various residents told him that his *Siebenbürger* accent reminded them of the way their great-great grandparents spoke.

In 1211[13], King Andrew II granted a special charter to the Teutonic Knights, under an order that was founded during the Third Crusade in 1189. The charter was to defend the land and convert the enemy, Tartars and Cumans, into Catholics, giving them the South-eastern region of Transylvania, which is also known as *Burzenland*. Their settlements though did not last long, as they were soon expelled from the Kingdom of Hungary after angering Andrew by proposing that the Pope Honorius III should have complete control over *Burzenland*.

After this disappointment, Andrew granted the Saxons complete self-governance, in 1124[14], under their own leader, the *Sachsen Graf* (the Saxon Count), as the German settlers seemed to be more trustworthy guests. Compared to other guest helpers, the Saxons were treated with a lot of respect and benefits. The *Goldene Freibrief* (Golden Charter), secured the Saxons with freedom and self-administration with the *Sachsen Graf* only being subject to the King. This allowed them enough freedom to develop and maintain their own culture, and customs in return of having certain military obligations. The *Goldene Freibrief* allowed the Saxons to elect their own clergymen and judges; their merchants were exempt from tolls and dues within the kingdom, in addition to the Saxons being able to own their own land and property. The freedom became one of the Saxons greatest strengths, and allowed them to keep their own religion and language. The *Goldene Freibrief* was still valid, in most parts, up until the early 20th century.

12   "ENCYCLOPAEDIA BRITANNICA." Corvinus Library - Hungarian History. Web. Nov. 2011. <http://www.hungarianhistory.com/lib/faf/toc06.htm>.
13   Hannover, Brigitta G. 'Rumaenien entdecken: Kunstschaetze und Naturschoenheiten'. (Berlin. Trescher-Reihe Reisen, 2007).p 119
14   ibit

Goldene Freibrief Andreas II from 1224 through King Kalr I. (1317)

As Harald v. Hochmeister (currently aged 78 and priest in Meschendorf from autumn 1961 to autumn 1968) states, during his time in Meschendorf, there was only the right of 'Freedom of Parish Election' remaining from the *Goldene Freibrief*. He also adds, that there was a down side to the 'freedom' given by the agreement towards the Saxons. The special agreement towards the Saxons compared to other ethnicities made the Saxons very proud.

The effects of Saxon pride were visible until the early 1900's. Harald v. Hochmeister states, "Stupidity and pride grow on the same wood". This had bad consequences for the Saxons. Families began to look at their own wealth, and tried to multiply this. As a result, they often only had one child, and then tried to increase their wealth though marriage by finding an appropriate partner.

In the mountainous areas of Transylvania, in the middle of the Carpathian Mountains, settlers brought with them various skills such as the ability to develop the region's economy and knowledge in agriculture, wine making and mining. Transylvania was made up of rich fertile lands and pastures along with valuable natural resources such as salts, precious minerals and red metal. Its ideal geographical location, allowed for trade routes at the west-east, and north-south junctions, resulting in various grid-like Saxon towns and villages flourishing. The Transylvanian villages were set up along with their German schools and Lutheran fortified Churches; resulting in a cultural autonomy, which was protected through hundreds of years through treaties with the respective ruling administration.

In addition to the Saxons, there were also other German speaking groups in Eastern Europe. Before 1918 Transylvania was under the Austrian-Hungarian monarchy where the government and bureaucracy was often run in German. After 1918 Transylvania was ruled under the nationalist government of Romania, which brought greater emphasis on the Saxons that their Saxonness related more to Germanness than any other culture, such as Romanian. After 1940 the Saxons were linked to greater Germany and the Third Reich, followed by the Romanian

L. Z.	Name, Vorname	Hausnr.	gefallen/ in Gefan-genschaft gestorben	vermißt	Truppeneinheit deutsch/rumänisch
12.	Galter Johann	19			deutsch
13.	Galter Georg	19			deutsch
14.	Galter Paul	19			deutsch
15.	Depner Martin	19			deutsch
16.	Töpfer Martin	20			deutsch
17.	Töpfer Johann	20	ja		deutsch
18.	Baier Michael	20			deutsch
19.	Töpfer Alfred	24			deutsch
20.	Depner Johann	25			deutsch
21.	Polder Michael	26			deutsch
22.	Baier Johann	27			deutsch
23.	Orendt Michael	27	ja		deutsch
24.	Schnell Martin	28			deutsch
25.	Schnell Johann	28	ja		deutsch
26.	Schuster Martin	29	ja		deutsch
27.	Depner Paul	30	ja		deutsch
28.	Schuster Friedrich	32	ja		rumänisch
29.	Schuster Paul	32			deutsch
30.	Schuster Johann	32	ja		rumänisch
31.	Konnerth Michael	33			deutsch
32.	Klein Martin	35		ja	deutsch
33.	Klein Johann	35	ja		deutsch
34.	Klein Georg	35			deutsch
35.	Klein Paul Robert	35			deutsch
36.	Deutschländer Martin	37			deutsch
37.	Deutschländer Johann	37			deutsch
38.	Deutschländer Petrus	37			deutsch
39.	Werner Johann, sen.	39	ja		deutsch
40..	Schmidt Rudolf	40			deutsch
41.	Schmidt Wilhelm	40			deutsch
42.	Roth Johann	41			deutsch
43.	Roth Paul	41	ja		deutsch
44.	Dörner Johann	102	ja		deutsch
45.	Töpfer August	104			deutsch
46.	Töpfer Georg	104			deutsch
47.	Schuster Andreas	109			deutsch
48.	Schuster Georg	109			deutsch

Residents in Meschendorf after WWII showing, Name, House Number, If they died during the War/In Prison Camp, gone missing, Troop they Fought it.

orientated communist regime in 1945 where the Germans were seen as the enemy and made responsible for the war, resulting in severe punishments. Some Saxons, and other Germans left Transylvania, but others were trapped behind the iron curtain. In 1989 the boarders were re-opened, but the National Romanian Government now ran Romania. Today, Romania is highly regulated by the E.U, and its borders are opened. Nevertheless the Saxons, and other Germans in Transylvania were attracted to stay in Germany as it allows for a better quality of life with its major economic power. Therefore one can see Meschendorf, as a micro society, in response to macro events.

The 1930's census shows the number of Saxons in Transylvania peaked, with 238,000 Saxons living in Transylvania. [15] Since then, the numbers have constantly decreased. Two main events triggered a mass exodus of Saxons from Transylvania: WWII and the fall of the communist dictator Ceausescu. During WWII it is believed that 175,000[16] Germans were either killed or had evacuated the country as a result of the war. A generation of young men were not able to return to Transylvania, which had become a communist country, resulting in many Saxon farms not having an heir. Since WWII many Saxons migrated to Germany or Austria, some moved as far as the USA, living mainly in Idaho, Ohio, Colorado or Canada within the Southern Ontario region. Many moved in hopes of finding a 'better' life, but those that wanted to return were unable to do so due to the Iron Curtain of the Communist regime not allowing for freedom of travel.

My grandfather was one of the many Saxons that was unable to return to Meschendorf after WWII. He was firstly enlisted into the Romanian army, initially allied with Germany, which later traded its German-speaking soldiers to the Nazi-German army. There, Georg, along with most other soldiers from Romania, was given the most dangerous duties in battle. He was sent to the *'Russland-Feldzug'*, where he was confronted by the Russian army, in Northeast Germany, at the river Elbe. The Russians won this battle, and George quickly swam over the Elbe to

---

15   1930 census shows around 750,000 Germans registered in Transylvaina; Transylvanian Saxons (238,000), Banater Swabian (280,000), Bukovina Germans (94,000), Bessarabia Germans (80,000), Sathmar Swabians (280,000), Dobrudja Germans (12,000).
16   Pettersen, Leif. Baker, Mark. 'Romania'. Lonely Planet 2010 p39

escape the Russian *Kriegsgefangenschaft*, which everyone assumed would surely have resulted in death. Georg was then captured by the US-Army who sent him of to a POW camp in Belgium. Upon his release he wished to return to his home in Meschendorf, but Meschendorf had now fallen under communist regime. If he were to return home, he would have been sent to one of the worst prison camps in Siberia known as *Gulag*. That way, Communist Romania demanded the Germans to compensate for damage done. For this reason he remained in Belgium, where he worked in mining until 1952 and later moved to his brother's house in Stuttgart, Germany where he met my Grandmother.

After WWII Romania became a Communist state, resulting in 70,000[17], Germans being accused of Nazi collaborations. As a punishment, Saxons were sentenced to 5-year in a hard labour camp. Therefore, straight after the war, many Saxons, being of German origin were transported to the Russian Gulag as they were seen as collaborators by the Communist regime.[18]

In addition to suffering from various accusations, those who returned from labour camp experienced two phases of nationalization which disowned the Saxons of the land they owned for over 800 years. This had a great impact on the rural Saxons, as farmland was all they owned. The nationalization also took away the Saxons autonomous community life, breaking up the tightly knitted cultural rules, as they went from being a self-regulated community to following the communist Romanian Government.

The higher prospects found in (then) West Germany, in addition to the Saxons cultural links with Germany, attracted ever more Saxons to emigrate. The decreasing number of Saxons in Transylvania wore away the will of the remaining Saxons to remain in Transylvania, where the ability to farm, and prosper was becoming increasingly difficult. As a result, since the early 1970's, two major waves of emigration occurred. This was also triggered by the more liberal emigration laws, which West Germany negotiated with the Romanian government. Germany

17   Riley, Bronwen. 'Transylvania'. (London. Frances Lincoln Limited, 2007 p61
18   See appendix Interview with Martin Klein.

was able to pay $8,000[19] US dollars for each exit permit and it is thought that by the 1980's around 70,000 exits for Saxons from Romania were "bought out" by Germany. With massive disparity in wealth between Germany and Romania, it did not take long after the collapse of the Ceausescu regime (Dec. 1989 to spring 1990), for half a million Saxons to pack up the few things they still owned and leave Romania through the newly opened borders.

As a result, currently less than 10%[20] of Saxon residents remain in Transylvania (compared to the early 1900's), turning history into memory. In Meschendorf, only one Saxon remains (aged 101).

19   Pettersen, Leif. Baker, Mark. 'Romania'. Lonely Planet 2010 p 39
20   "Building Sustainably by Learning from Traditional Architecture." INTBAU -
International Network for Traditional Building, Architecture & Urbanism. Web. Sep. 2011.
<http://www.intbau.org/archive/courses.htm>.

Cheese served in Martin Kleins Summer Kitchen.
Photograph: Meschendorf 2011

ARRIVAL IN MESCHENDORF

Flying over Hermannstadt (one of the largest Saxon towns in Transylvania, also known as Sibiu (in Romanian)) there was sunshine on the left side of the airplane, but when looking to the right, the sky was covered with dark clouds and rain was striking the ground. This was almost a sign of the extreme opposites I was about to encounter in the Saxon villages of Transylvania, Romania. The picturesque fairytale image that Meschendorf portrayed, juxtaposed with its darker corrupted politics, and reminder of the communist era.

I arrived in Meschendorf as the moon's glow replaced the suns shine. A six kilometer country road, paved for the first time last year, lead to the lower part of the village, where small houses owned by Romanian settlers who arrived in the late 1940's could be found. There are no streetlights in Meschendorf, and although locals do have electricity, it is scarcely used due to its energy costs. I found myself in front of an unlit house, which I identified from a past photograph as the house of Martin Klein, my grandfathers brothers son, aged 74. Martin generously invited me to stay in his Meschendorf house during my visit. No one answered when knocking, so I decided to enter the unlit courtyard. Suddenly I heard the sounds of a horse carriage rumbling down the Meschendorf cobbled, wide *Mittelgasse* (main street) about ten metres away from where I was standing. I saw nothing but a silhouette passing through the darkness in which I found myself. I noticed another silhouette approaching the house, this time it was Martin. He had just been down to the cheese 'shop', owned by the local sheep farmer who sells goods from his own home.

Straight away I was lead into the courtyard to a table set in the summer kitchen. It was a warm August evening. I was served with three different flavoured cheeses, all made the same way, but tasted very differently due to the time when they were produced. The freshest cheese was twenty minutes old, the second was made five hours ago and the

From the left: My Grandfathers House, Martin Kleins House, Neighbours House
Photograph: Meschendorf Summer 1980

third was made the previous day, it was amazing to see how things changed so fast just through time.

To drink I was served *Schnaps*, which is a traditional alcoholic beverage, served in shot glasses, but drunk by locals as if it were water. *Schnaps* is made by distilling fruits such as plums or apples and tends to have an alcoholic content of around 40%-90%. Many Saxons distilled their own *Schnaps* within their homes from collected plums or apples, often found growing along the Saxon village roads. There was a choice between cold or warm *Schnaps*. The warm *Schnaps* was heated with caraway seeds and sugar. After a while though I was desperate to ask for a glass of water, I was not accustomed to the harsh taste and customs.

During dinner we discussed aspects of ownership of the houses and land in Meschendorf. A topic that was brought up by most Saxons I encountered throughout my visit. During the Communist era the Saxons lost ownership of their land and homes, with no guarantee of re-possessing it even after the collapse of Communism. Although the new restitution laws allow Saxons to regain ownership of their houses and land, many Saxons still struggle validating this law. The regulations are very complicated, and the bureaucracy is not always forthcoming. There are various factors, which make the process difficult. Not all property ownership was documented in the land registry prior to the Communist era, in addition there is also a law stating that to gain ownership back of ones home and land, one must have Romanian citizenship. When the Saxons entered Germany though, it was mandatory for them to adopt German citizenship, and give up their Romanian one, as dual citizenship was not permitted. Emotionally, that was what they aspired to anyway.

Nevertheless, it is important to consider other factors for why the Saxon rural villages are disappearing. Although, especially the elderly have nostalgic connections to their place of birth, they enjoy much better living conditions in a more developed capitalist society. Relocating back to Meschendorf would only offer them a difficult farmers' life, which

most people would struggle with. Also, the amount of Saxons in the villages has decreased to a critical point, where the historic life, in a tightly knitted community, with old customs, and rituals is inevitably no longer possible. Therefore, Meschendorf, like many other Saxon villages, has become a 'holiday' destination for its past Saxon residents rather than a village of settled, permanent Saxons. When Saxons return to Meschendorf for the summer, they may be able to enjoy delightful memories of the past, but struggle to maintain what they owned, with the constant need to renovate buildings that are hundreds of years old.

However, some Saxon villages show that wise investment into "Nostalgia" can help revitalize the past; *Weisskirch* (also known as Viscri in Romanian), a neighbouring Saxon village, 14 km from Meschendorf seems to have managed to get some of its past Saxon residents back, by having an income through tourism. Various houses were renovated with the aid of the Mihai-trust. The main attraction is the fortified Saxon church, which is equipped with a museum, making it a tourist target for those who want to experience Saxon history.

Although *Weisskich* is as remotely located as Meschendorf, Meschendorf has not managed to attract many tourists. Against the backdrop of its impressive, but collapsing buildings, most of Meschendorfs residents comprise of Romanians and Romas who struggle to meet their own financial needs.

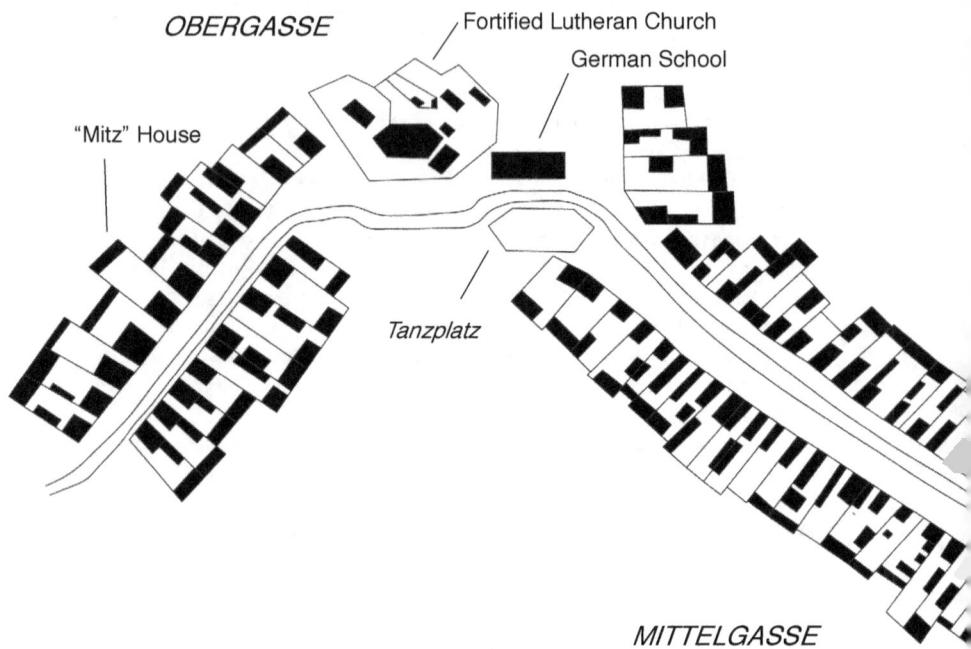

OBERGASSE

Fortified Lutheran Church

German School

"Mitz" House

Tanzplatz

MITTELGASSE

Sketch drawing of Meschendorf.
no responsibility taken for accuracy.

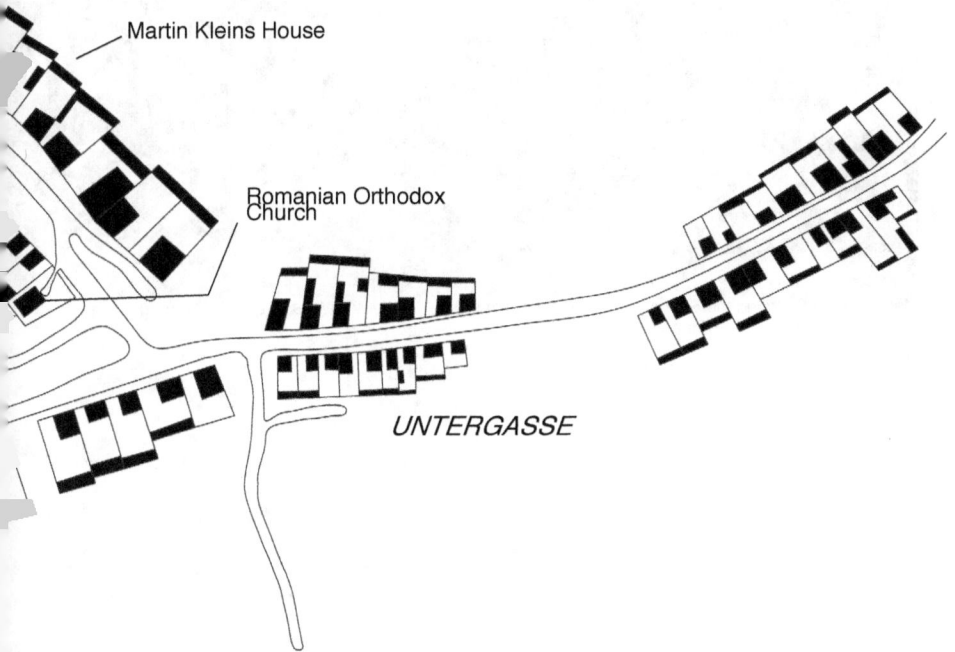

Martin Kleins House

Romanian Orthodox
Church

UNTERGASSE

Meschendorf Showing the Saxon Lutheran Church at the top of the *Mittelgasse*, and the Romanian Orthodox Church at the lower part of the *Mittelgasse*.

Meschendorf is one of the most beautiful Saxon villages. Set up around 1150,[21] the village was originally named Messendorf in the 14th century, which later evolved to Mesche and then Meschendorf. It is one of the few villages that sound similar in Saxon-german 'Meschendorf' and its Romanian name 'Meşendorf'. The first historical documentation was made in 1289[22]. Throughout history, the village has been destroyed multiple times through fires; in 1469, 1641, 1755 and 1804.[23]

Like most Saxon villages, Meschendorf is made up of a single wide mud backed street with houses aligned on either side. Saxon villages were built the same way for centuries, even the newer houses built after WWII remain unchanged. Often a stream runs down the side of the street aligned with fruit trees, such as apples, plums and pears. Animals such as ducks and geese waddle along the road, with the odd dog resting in front of its owner's home, paying close guard.

The street in Meschendorf is divided into three parts *Obergasse*, *Mittelgasse* and *Untergasse*. The *Obergasse* is the highest point, leading to the *Mittelgasse* from the Saxon fortified Church downwards until the newer Orthodox Romanian church, and finishing on the margins of the village with the *Untergasse* which mainly houses brightly dressed Romanian and Roma citizens. Currently only around 150 of the 250 remaining Saxon houses in Meschendorf are inhabited, though no longer by Saxons but by Romanians or Romas.

Memories, and experiences related to culture, traditions and architecture are discussed from the upper part of the village *Obergasse* down to the lower part of the village *Untergasse*. This will be done through discussions with past Saxon residents, relating their experiences, combined with historical facts to architecture found along this route, starting with the Saxon home, followed by the eldest remaining Saxon resident in Meschendorf who lives in the Obergasse, the Fortified Church, German School, *Tanzplatz, Mittelgasse* and finishing at the lower part of the village

21   "Building Sustainably by Learning from Traditional Architecture." INTBAU - International Network for Traditional Building, Architecture & Urbanism. Web. Sep. 2011. <http://www.intbau.org/archive/courses.htm>.
22   "Whole Village Projects Mesendorf-Meschendorf -Mese." The Mihai Emines-cu Trust. 2002. Web. Sept. 2011. <http://www.mihaieminescutrust.org/content/nd_village.asp?n=97>.
23   ibit

Wood Joint
Photograph: Meschendorf 2011

Untergasse with the Romanian Orthodox Church where the 'new' Romanian and Roma residents have mainly settled. The *Mittelgasse* is the widest part of the street. There used to be a great ditch in front of the houses from the top of the street all the way to the end, through which a stream of water flowed. Every second neighbouring house had one bridge to access their home. This was to reduce the amount of excess bridges. In the 1880's Meschendorf made a lot of money through selling timber oak with which they could afford to build their community hall, *Tanzplatz*, construct their water system (including 3 water troughs) and also fill in the ditch to create a 'flat' cobbled street.

Although various writers compare the Transylvanian Saxon villages to those of the English countryside 100 -200 years ago, they are more likely to mirror villages found in the Mosel area of Germany. Saxon houses have Dutch gables, which possibly give a clue to their northern origins. The houses are often painted in pastel colours of green, yellow or pale blue, in contrast with the Romanian houses painted stronger, darker colours. Saxon houses are built in a simple style with little ornament, and small windows, resulting in the facade looking like a defence wall. This impression is amplified as houses are built very close to each other, with a large front wall and gate to keep out foreigners and protect against attack. In a similar way, the churches consist of massive towers and walls, once used for defence purposes at times of war.

All Saxon houses were constructed using natural, locally sourced materials with the aid of neighbours. The ground floor of the main house was built directly onto the soil without any foundations. The walls were constructed out of clay and stone (since the 1400's). The clay was used directly from the earth, ground, and mixed with water. The houses were built stone on stone, with the clay only functioning to fill the gaps rather than being applied as a thick layer. This created a firm 60-80 cm thick wall keeping houses cool in summer and warm in winter.

The columns and beams in Saxon houses were built inside the houses, but outside the walls (on the interior side). This is because the walls would often be damp,

A Saxon House has the Name of its Inhabitants, and Last Renovation Date Written on the Dutch Gable.
Photograph: Meschendorf 2011

A Saxon House inscription rhyme in Meschendorf
" This House is only made of, Sand and Stone, But yet I can not stay here Forever. 19 M.u.
G Hch. 1988"
- a reference that the Saxons can not remain forever in their Home in Meschendorf.
Photograph: Meschendorf 2011

leading the wood to rot. Therefore the Saxons developed a system where the columns had as minimal as possible contact with the walls, and would always be aired out. As a wood joinery, carefully hand crafted wooden nails were used. Unfortunately today, the highly exposed beams are frequently stolen and sold on to antique dealers.

Saxon houses traditionally have the last renovation date, and name of the inhabitant written on the Dutch gables, on the exterior front façade. It is very easy to detect if Romanians now live in a Saxon house, as the name and date would be replaced by a cross, a symbol of the Romanian Orthodox Church. It was also very common for Saxon houses to have a 'roof with eyes'. This was a large circular window in the Dutch gable, which functioned as a light source into the storage space directly underneath the roof of the house.

It appears as though the Saxon houses are continuously aligned on either side of the street, but on closer observation one realises that they do not have their house entrance facing the street. Instead, a massive gate, of equal height to the house wall blocks off the inner courtyard with its access to the house. Therefore to enter a Saxon house, one must first pass through a small door cut into the front gate, to reach the inner courtyard, which then gives access to the house. The Saxon house, similar to its church, was designed to keep the Saxons to themselves, securing their privileges and making access for foreigners difficult.

This illustrates how Saxons prefer to keep a closed community rather than relating and mixing with other cultures living in Transylvania such as the Hungarians and Romanians. Saxons created a secretive life, which was only shared and experienced within their own community. Although Romanians often lived in Saxon villages they would only settle at the border of the villages, and would only be able to do simpler jobs such as being a herdsman, or help with cleaning and maintaining the farm. In the case of Meschendorf, the Romanians would live on the *Untergasse*, the lower part of the village.

Behind the large front gate, lays everything a family required to survive. At the far end of the

Saxon Bed 'drawers' were pulled apart every evening to accommodate
more than one Person.
Photograph: Weisskirch Saxon Museum 2011.

inner courtyard were pens for chickens and a *Scheune* (barn) for pigs, cows and sheep. A second large barn stored the tools, hay and wood for heating and cooking. A vegetable garden provided the basic needs for food, in addition to a far larger orchard and field behind the barn for grazing. Many families even had their own water well; others used the public wells provided along the street. As summers in this region tend to be very hot, a summer kitchen located near the family home was the central point of activity within the household. It was located at the exterior of the home, to keep the house smoke free and clean.

A Saxon house is very small, using every space to its maximum potential. The ground floor is approximately 1.8m in height and functioned as the cellar, which was used as storage for wheat, barley, potatoes, sauerkraut, and wine. The seven to nine stairs, located at the side of the house, lead into the first floor, which functioned as the main house. The main house is made up of two rooms, of approximately 2.2 – 2.4 m in height, which are connected through an oven that also functions as heating. The smaller room, *Aufenthaltsraum* was the most used, as it contained the kitchen, beds and weaving stool. The larger room was used for celebrations. The space beneath the roof was used to dry corn, and the washing.

A traditional Saxon bed can be described as a chest of draws that was pulled apart every evening, and stacked back upright for the daytime due to the lack of space within a Saxon home. Often entire families would sleep in a single room, each having their space within a different level of the Saxon bed. It was tradition that the newly married couple would take the top part of the bed, whereas the children would take the smallest and lowest part. It was not uncommon that a newly wed couple would sleep in the same room as the parents/in-laws until they had their own space they could call home. More often more than one generation though would share a house.

This shows the lack of privacy and personal space Saxons had. Not even couples had their own private

Top: Martin Kleins House, view from the courtyard (*Scheune*).
Bottom: Martin Kleins *Scheune* (barn), view fom the House.
Photograph: Meschendorf 2011

space, and everything had to be shared on minimal space.

The set up of a Saxon house shows that the rural Saxons lived a very simple life, with very few possessions, let alone luxuries. Most activities were work related and took place outside of the home, mainly on the fields. Everyone would work together creating a strong community, although as later discussed it was compulsory to work and support each other, as this was strongly monitored by the *Nachbarschaft,* the Saxon way of ruling its villages, which was followed by punishments if a Saxon did not oblige with these rules. This can be seen as a strange mix of voluntary and forced actions.
Both neighbouring Saxon houses were built with a similar layout. A Saxon was always responsible for the land division on the left side of his/her house, facing from the streets. Therefore he/she was always responsible on closing of his/her border to the neighbouring property.
Fields extended out from the back of the village up to the woodland. The land was divided into various strips, similar to that of medieval Europe. Each family owned more than one strip of land, which was often located distances apart. Different crops would be farmed on each strip of field according to the soil quality and where the land was lying. Unlike the rest of Europe, this method of strip farming was maintained in the villages, until the communist era. Livestock was able to graze freely on communal meadows that were not controlled by fences but by shepherds and cowherds.
To maximise the land use, steep areas were transformed into terraces where cereal, vegetable and vines for wine were grown. Meschendorf used to be surrounded by various vine terraces, which are now overgrown by wild flowers.
During the communist era the spacious orchard behind the *Scheue* was cut back due to "socialisation". The *Scheune* was moved forward towards the house, reducing the space of the inner courtyard. Many farmers decided to move the *Scheune* from the far end of their inner courtyard towards the main house as they no longer required the space for personal farming.

QUOTATIONS FROM AN ARTICLE PUBLISHED IN 1926 BY DR. KARL WOLFF OF HERMANNSTADT "Today, things are different. Under the title "Agrarian Reform", the Rumanian authorities have taken away from the Saxon communities many thousands of acres of fields, meadows, woods and pastures compensating them with ridiculously low prices[24]; so the loss of Saxon property is running up into the billions of Lei. Even very small estates of Saxons were expropriated. Two women of Billak, whose husbands were totally disabled in the war, lost their small properties-one plot of six acres, the other of eight acres - by the act of expropriation. The seizure was justified on the grounds that the land was acquired as late as 1921. "][25]

Unfortunately, when Martin moved his *Scheune* towards his home, the land behind the *Scheune* was taken over during the communist time, for the forced, but often not efficiently functioning larger communal farms. The idea was that rather than everyone having their own farmland, and stock, the entire village would create a larger farm where everyone would work together. This was not successful as everyone put greater emphasis on what they had left under private ownership, rather than to make function what was being shared.
    This phenomenon can be related back to the previously discussed idea that the Saxon, although appearing to work together within the community also had a strong tendency to keep his own wealth to himself. Therefore the idea of shared farming without ownership did not appeal to the Saxon way of life, as personal profit could not be made.
    Saxon villages, in comparison to Romanian villages, showed strong confidence and relative wealth. Romanians generally built with wood, due to lack of money, skill and resources to build out of stone, resulting in a lack to defend themselves. Romanians were constantly afraid of being under attack, that in some parts of the country, they even constructed their churches on wheels to move them to safety. This method was also put in use in the 1980's[26], when some of Bucharest's

---

24   "About 1% of the value of land" according to John M. Cabot's "The Racial Conflict in Transylvania" p 74
25   Foisel, John. 'Saxons through the Seventeen Centuries: A history of the Transyvanian Saxons'. (Cleveland, Ohio. Central Alliance of Transylvanian Saxons in the United States, 1936.) p 303
26   Riley, Bronwen. 'Transylvania'. (London. Frances Lincoln Limited, 2007 p 32.

historic churches were under threat by the Communist President Ceausescu. The Mihai Voda[27] church was moved on wheels, but only succeeded a few hundred metres before larger apartment blocks obstructed its passageway.

This is a contrast compared to the Saxon churches which were constructed out of heavy stonewalls to function as a defence mechanism, and provide protection rather than having to be protected.

Romanian houses also did not show the same obsession of defence, and privacy compared to Saxon houses. It is possible to view the courtyard of a Romanian house, even if some contain gates, making the connection between the house and the exterior very open.

27   Riley, Bronwen. 'Transylvania'. (London. Frances Lincoln Limited, 2007
p 32.

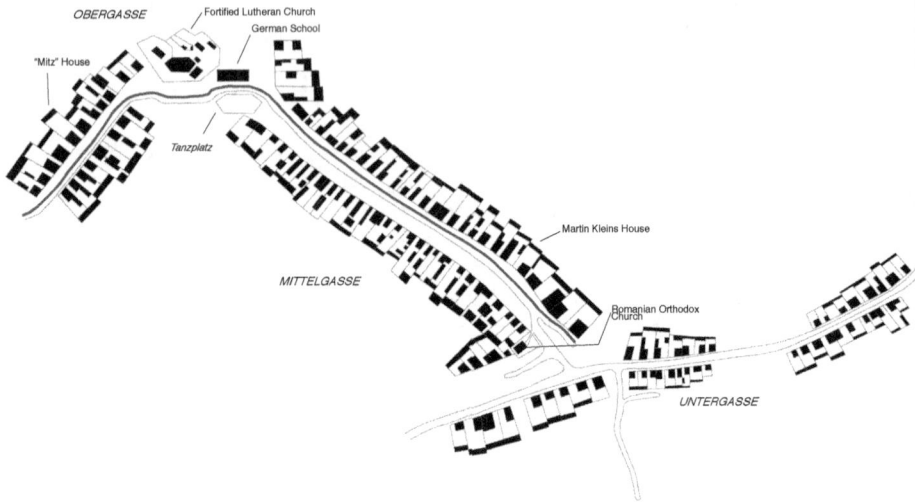

OBERGASSE Fortified Lutheran Church
German School
"Mitz" House
Tanzplatz
Martin Kleins House
MITTELGASSE
Romanian Orthodox
Church
UNTERGASSE

Martin Werner
"Mitz"

OBERGASSE

Fortified Lutheran
Church

Old German School Building
now Abandoned

MITTELGASSE

Renovated
community hall

Sold to Romanians

Martins Grandfa
have Church ins
Romanian State gave   Used by
home to Romanian family "Saturday Belie"
with Children   1989

Johan Konnert   Expropriated
Carpenter lived here till 1920   Martin Klein   Family left to Germany
then moved to Germany   built 1963, Land Newly renovated and u
                        Georg Klein   was expropriated Holiday home by Hans
                                      till 1956

sed to be Town Hall
t now is used as
chool with 4 grades

Was meant to be
Church, but no
funding

Hostel sponsored by Muttenz
(partner town in Switzerland)
Almost no visitors

Martin
left to Germany

Aunt Traenchen still
owns it but Romas live
inside.

an
ovated

Collapsed house

Collapsed house

Romanian families
home already prior to
WWII. (M.E.T renovated
facade)

Re-built
1963

Expropriated-
German family lived
with a Romanian
amily who made oil
rom sunflowers

Before 1940- shop
"Letches" selling sugar
and Schnaps

Werner

Schmidt Wilhelm
Expropriated

'Mitz' aged 101, the last Saxon remaining in Meschendorf.
Photograph: Meschendorf 2011

OBERGASSE

___HOUSE OF MITZ, AGED 101

At the highest point of the *Obergasse*, lives Martin Werner aged 101, the last remaining Saxon resident in Meschendorf. Within the Meschendorf community he is known as 'Mitz'. He lives in the same house he had lived in for the past 70 years (a house which was built in the 1700's and was since then renovated), with the aid of his Romanian care takers, a very highly thought of family in Meschendorf. Over a period of 50 years, Mitz worked at the church as church father and church curator in addition to playing the trombone in the *Blaskapelle* (Brass band). He states that he did not leave Meschendorf in the late 1980's when most Saxon residents left, as he was already in his 80's at that time, proclaiming that he was born there, christened there, educated there, married there and therefore should also die there in Meschendorf. This is a reflection of the strong roots that the Meschendorfer Saxons have built into their hometown, and also reflects the feelings of nostalgia most Saxons that have left Meschendorf, feel today.

I asked Mitz if he is still in contact with the Saxons that have left Meschendorf. He describes how he was given a surprise 100th birthday party, on the 4th of July 2010, (although his birthday is on the 2nd of July it was held on Sunday the 4th after the church service). Many Meschendorfer Saxons attended this special re-union, travelling from Germany. His birthday was mentioned after the church service had taken place, which made him feel very honoured and proud, especially after his long history of working within the church. The past *Blaskapelle* (Brass band), which played a major role in community events, also travelled from Germany in honour of his birthday, and performed in the church. The church had finally been filled again with a variety of people, and many tables with food were set up in the courtyard- a scene that those who attended remember as an experience "just like in the old days"

Das Stufenalter des Mannes: 1900's drawing of the Ideal stages of man in relation to his age

As to his age Mitz says that there is no one else, in Meschendorf, that made it to 101, which makes him very proud, and yet now that everyone has left Meschendorf he feels very alone. He describes how he sometimes stands at his window for half the day. Where he would have been able to watch various people in the past, there now walks no one apart from a possible flock of geese. He contemplates on what he is still doing here in Meschendorf. A human that is alone, cannot speak to anyone, and lives a very lonely life. And yet he cannot let go of his home ground. His plan for the rest of his life is a simple one, to eat and drink what he can.

In his home hangs a traditional drawing *Das Stufenalter des Mannes* (The step age of the man) that portrays a mans ideal achievements and priorities in relationship to his age. Mitz's age stands on the last Pedi stool stating "100 Jahre. Und dann wenn hundert Jahr vorbei, Bet'er dass Gott im gnaedig sei" (100 years. And when one hundred years have passed, he asks for gods mercy)

Mitz starts to describe Meschendorf from when he was a child. According to Mitz, poverty was already present in Meschendorf before the communist time. During WWI Saxons had suffered from a great blow of poverty, which resulted in Meschendorfer Saxons only being able to wear what the woman managed to weave and sew from the locally grown hemp. To eat they had the meats from the livestock, and other produce made within the community. It was not until the 1930's that Meschendorf was supplied with electricity, nor did they have oil to burn. Instead lard from the pigs was placed into a turnip with a wick that was lit alight to create a 'candle'. Meschendorfer Saxons also did not have enough money to buy items such as pure salt. Therefore salt water was used as a substitute. It was also possible to obtain salt (with dirt) from the stones in the surrounding hills, which had to be filtered for purification. The state of poverty continued throughout the communist era, as all goods were rationed until the 70's.

Martin Werner describes the time when Meschendorf was ruled by communism. There was a *Kolchose*, a state-

owned agricultural farm where each farmer had to work
for a share of the Produce. Private ownership of land
was limited to very small plots, but as the state-
owned farm was not well organized, it was down to
each individual how much he or she contributed to the
Kolchose results. On a daily basis it was recorded how
many hours, and in what field one was working. It was
Mitzs responsibility to herd the Oxen, and cows and
managed the chickens. Work was not paid through money,
instead rations Norm were given which in return could
be traded for food, clothing etc. This new system of
communal farming in a centralised shared space had a
huge impact on the agricultural landscape surrounding
the village. The hills around Meschendorf used to be
divided into various individual farms ranging from
cowherds to vine fields. Through the *Kolchose* the small
fields merged together creating fewer larger fields.
The terraced vineyards were gradually replaced with
cattle grazing grounds. In addition the aspirations
of the individual farmers to work for their own
produce was replaced by a centrally run system
where "the plan" ruled the priorities of the work.
   The underlying idea of the state farms was to create
massive industrial production schemes rather than
everyone working on their own farmland. Everyone in
the village was allocated a job on the farm according
to their talents and capabilities. However the system
turned out to be very inefficient, as each individual put
greater emphasis on what they personally still owned.
   Although communist state organised farming
was inefficient in most communities, it was
particularly difficult for the Saxons to adapt to
this system. For over 800 years the Saxon farming
community had been built on private ownership,
autonomous farming, and a self-regulatory system
in community life. They were not adjusted to follow
rules that came from outside the Saxon community.

"This soil we have created for ourselves,
By the hard labour of our hands; we've changed
The giant forest, that was erst the haunt
Of savage bears, into a home for men;
Extirpated the dragon's blood, that wont
To rise, dissent with venom, from the swamps;
Rent the thick mystic canopy that hung
Its blighting vapors on the dreary waste;
Blasted the soil rock; o'er the abyss
Thrown the firm bridge for the wayfaring man;-
By the possession of a thousand years
This soil is ours….
And shall an alien lord
Himself a vassal, dare to venture here,
on our own hearths insult us,- and attempt
To do us shame on our own proper soil?
Is there no help against such wrong as this?"

- Schiller

After the revolution, and the fall of communism most remaining Saxons left Meschendorf and immigrated to Germany. Mitz explains that during communism, as mentioned, the animals were taken away from individual ownership, everything was taken away but one could not leave. Therefore, as soon as the possibility of 'escape' emerged, everyone took advantage of it. If a Saxon were to obtain his land back, how should he possibly be able to farm it? The Saxons no longer owned any lively stock, not to mention tools or money, as all hard work had been paid with rations. "If you were a simple person or rich, life was a battle."

Speck tower where the ham was hung and protected within the Fortified Church walls.
Above: Photograph: Meschendorf 1980
Below: Photograph: Meschendorf 2011

Previous Page:
Lutheran Church, looking up from the Mittelgasse.
Photograph: Meschendorf 2011

THE FORTIFIED CHURCH

The Lutheran Church is the highest centre point within
Meschendorf and is a great reminder of its flourishing
and culturally active past. It was built in the 1350's[28]
over a period of 200 years located where the *Obergasse*
and *Mittelgasse* meet. The church played a major role in
the Saxon villages as it replaces the Noble mans castle,
in times of war, as a defence with its high protective
stone wall and large towers overlooking the village.

The Saxon church was not only the centre point for
religious gatherings and festivities, but also housed
the local grinding mill in addition to being storage
for foods such as grain and speck. Everyone within
the community used the grinding mill and thresher
stored within the church walls. The thresher was
passed from house to house to grind goods. Fruit trees
were planted within the defence walls, in addition
to having storage for grain to provide provisions in
difficult times. The grain would be stored in wooden
boxes kept within the inner walls, underneath an
overlying projecting wooden tiled roof, protecting
the grain from both rain and weapons. A well provided
water, and meats and ham were dried and stored within
the *Speckturm*. All locals hung the speck or ham within
the church tower *Speckturm*. This tradition originated
from the historic past where Saxons were constantly
under threat. Therefore, all foods were stored within
the church walls, as provisions in times of emergency.

In an instance of attack, Saxons would flee to the
inside walls of the church, and would have sufficient
food to survive for days. Although this dates back
hundreds of years ago, the tradition of having the
speck in the tower remained until the 1900's. Even in
the 1900's, it was still only possible to have access
to ones speck on Sundays. Everyone who wished to cut
some of his or her own speck for the upcoming week
would have to ask the church father for permission to
access the church tower. So that no one stole speck
from anyone else, each resident had their own metal
stamp that they would imprint into the freshly cut

---

28   Topfer, Friedrich. 'Meschendorf am Steinberg'. (Nuernberg. Siebenbuer-
grisch-Sachsische Stiftung, 2000) p 9

Hanging *Speck* within Church Tower.
Photograph: Weisskirch.2011

speck to mark that it was they who cut the last piece. Nevertheless there were still occasions where people blamed others that their speck had been cut. This once again shows how each Saxon was very protective, and almost paranoid over the few belongings they owned.

When visiting the fortified church I was able to climb up the church tower, where I was able to view the entire village. A fragile spiralling decaying ladder, held together by sticks as thin as 2 cm lead to the top. There were no rails to hold on to, and missing floorboards allowed me to see from the top down to the bottom. From the top of the Lutheran Church one is able to see two graveyards, one belonging to the Lutheran Church, the other to the presently more active Romanian Orthodox Church. The Lutheran Church's' graveyard is very different to that of the Orthodox Church located approximately a 10-minute walk from one another. The most poignant difference is that the Lutheran graveyard is concreted, as there are hardly any Saxons remaining to maintain the flower beds, which were flourishing and well maintained in the past. The Orthodox Church is located in the lower part of village where the *Untergasse* starts, and caters for the Romanian and Roma residents.

Church services were held every Sunday. A Saxons position within the church was a symbol of status within the village. Similar to the Romanian Orthodox church, men and woman were segregated into different areas. In the front rows, near the choir, sat the children and unmarried girls, which was then followed by the married woman. Unmarried men were kept at a distance in the back gallery space whereas the married men were allowed to sit in the aisle on either side. This was to avoid any temptations that were taboo in the Saxon community.

Within the church, at eye level to the pastor, next to the pulpit hung a sand timer. Saxons lived on a very tight schedule where as much work as possible had to be done. Therefore the sand timer was to make sure that the pastor would not run over his time. This can be compared to the German stereotype of precision with time and a strong work ethic.

Interior of the Meschendofer Lutheran Church showing Saxon Tapestries, pulpit, altar with Organ.
Photograph: Meschendorf, Martin Eicher 1995

Mitz describes how, when Meschendorf still had its Saxon residents, everyone would aid one another. One example of this was the renovations of the Church that were necessary after the earthquake in the 70's. He states, "Everyone helped out in the re-building process, even the woman". Nowadays there is hardly anyone left in the church, just thorns and stinging nettles. He describes how, when he still had his strength, he removed the weeds from the church for over 15 years, as he could not bare the look of the church being overgrown. This is a reference to the reality that a community that was once there, now isn't, and even the plants are pushing their way through the remaining architecture.

The Saxons not only enjoyed political freedom, but also religious freedom, as Transylvania was one of the unique areas that went through a bloodless Reformation. The Catholic Church, giving all clergy men noble status, equally accepted most religions, Lutheran Saxon, Calvinist and Unitarian Hungarians. Unfortunately, the Orthodox Romanian church, to which most Romanian citizens belong, was not recognized, and therefore did not gain these privileges. This shows how the Romanians, although living in their own country were the less privileged group.

The Saxon Lutheran Church played a major role in the Saxons identity, as it was the main power, which also controlled the school system. The power of the Lutheran Church strongly decreased after WWII.

"The Church took over many tasks, ascribed to it by the newly created situation. The autonomy that the nation had within the state was vested in it. That was salient first of all in the fields connected with preserving the specificity of the Saxon people. Since the Church was the carrier of the German schooling system and it had to defend it against the Magyarisation efforts, its job was to preserve German language and culture. (Binder, "Die Evangelische Kirche" 238)][29]

---

29   Cercel, C. "The relationship between religious and national identity in the case of Transylvanian Saxons (1933-1944)" Nationalities papers. Vol 39, No. 2. 2011: p136

From: Fabritius Dancia Juliana
Saxon Fortified Churches in Siebenbuergen, Hermannstadt 1983

During, and after WWI various items within the community and church were stolen. Mitz describes how in WWI two of the largest church bells were stolen to make weapons, such as cannons out of the melted metal. In 1923 these two bells were then replaced by the big church bell, which currently still exists within the church tower. It is also said by Mitz that the school bell was also under threat to be taken by the communists in the mid 1900's. As a result it was hidden within the church by one of the Saxons. After the revolution, Hans, a past Meschendorfer Saxon took the school bell to a safe place in Nurnberg, Germany where it can still be found today.

Zahl 1/874.

Stempelfrei nach Tarifpost 22, e.

Elementar-Volksschul-Zeugnis.

Christian Töpfer _____, geboren

in _Mese_ , _____ Komitat, am

7. März 1 _864_, Schüler des _IX_. Jahrganges an

der evang. Elementarvolksschule A. B. in _Mese_, erhält über das

Schuljahr 18_78/79_ die allgemeine Zeugnisklasse _erste_.

Sittliches Betragen _____
Fleiß . . . . _____

Leistungen in den einzelnen Unterrichtsgegenständen:

Religions- und Sittenlehre (nach dem Zeugnisse eines Religionslehrers) _____

Magyarische Sprache:
  Sprechübungen . . . .
  Lesen . . . .
  Sprachlehre . . . .
  Rechtschreiben . . . .
  Lesestücke { Geläufiges Lesen . . . .
             Erörterung des Inhaltes
  Aufsatzübungen . . . .
Deutsche Sprache:
  Lesen . . . .
  Rechtschreiben . . . .
  Aufsatzübungen . . . .
Rechnen . . . .
Geometrie . . . .
Geographie . . . .
Geschichte . . . .
Bürgerliche Rechte und Pflichten .
Naturgeschichte . . . .
Naturkunde und Chemie . . . }
Schönschreiben . . . .
Gesang . . . .
Zeichnen . . . .
Turnen . . . .
Landwirtschaft { Theorie . .
              Praxis . .
Handarbeiten . . . .

Versäumte Halbtage (Stunden) _____ Davon entschuldigt wegen Krankheit _____ , wegen anderer

Ursachen _____ , nicht entschuldigt _____

Hat er (sie) magyarisch gelernt und in welchem Maße? _____

Mese am 5. Juli 1914.

_____ (Vorstand des Schulstuhls).

_____ Klassenlehrer.

Andeutung der Zeugnisstufen:
a) für das Sittliche Betragen:
1 = vollkommen angemessen
2 = angemessen
3 = minder angemessen
b) für den Fleiß:
1 = lobenswert
2 = nicht genügend
c) für die Leistungen in den Unterrichtsgegenständen und die allgem. Zeugnisklasse:
1 = ausgezeichnet
2 = vorzüglich
3 = gut
4 = hinreichend
5 = nicht hinreichend.

Volksschulzeugnis (1914),
Christian Töpfer.

Elementary School Reportcard (1914), Christian Toepfer

___GERMAN SCHOOL

Just next to the fortified church lies a large building that used to function as the German School. The school was built in 1888 from stones taken from the fortified church wall, when it no longer had to be of a certain height to function as a defence.[30] Today, the school is no more than an abandoned building that can no longer support the glass planes within its crooked window frames.

The ground floor of the school used to be the Kindergarten, which was run by Frau Marianna Stoian, whereas the second floor contained two schoolrooms and a teacher's office. This was reduced to only one of the schoolrooms being used for children grade 1-4 with the staff continuously changing until the German School was totally abandoned. Thanks to support from Muttenz, a partner town located in Switzerland, the school building was renovated both internally and externally in addition to being supplied with heating along with donations of toys for the kindergarten. Nevertheless the history and memories, which the heavy stones of the building carry within, have not been lost.

To the left of the school was the entrance to a youth club, which was constructed in 2003 for the Romanian and Roma youths but closed in 2005. The space was initially designed for young people to meet in a heated space, but unfortunately there were frequent problems of sound disturbance and alcohol leading to its closure. Today the space is transformed into a Post Office, which is run by Doina Scoica, who is one of the few locals left that still carries with her the knowledge of the towns past language, German, although she is not a Saxon. The constant changes of the buildings purpose are almost a reflection of the changes of culture, and citizens within Meschendorf.

---

30   Toepfer, Friedrich. 'Meschendorf am Steinberg'. (Nuernberg. Siebenbuer-grisch-Sachsische Stiftung, 2000) p9

Previous Page:
Tanzplatz
Photograph: Meschendorf 2011

___TANZPLATZ

The culture centre *Tanzplatz* (place of dance) is
located opposite and slightly below the old German
School building, marking the highest point of the
Mittelgasse. The *Tanzplatz* is the largest open meeting
ground in the village, and hosted most of the historic
events and traditions. It is constructed on promontory,
which today only overlooks the emptiness and poverty
of the village. The space used to function as a
meeting ground for cultural events such as theatre,
music or dance. Nowadays it is hardly ever used, but
is still available for baptism ceremonies or weddings.

When entering the space one is confronted with
stillness and silence, with just the memory of the
spaces past creating dances and sounds purely existing
within ones mind. It is like entering a circus without
an act going on. An eerie feeling of knowing that
the space should be filled with sound and joy rather
than feeling the coldness of the grey stone walls
that are falling apart, and standing alone, with only
the beating of wind and rain paying regular visits.

One of the many festivals held at the *Tanzplatz* was
Pfingsten (Whitsun), which could best be described as
judgement day. It originated from a Christian festival,
which celebrates the rise of the Holy Spirit, 50 days
after Easter. Before the Second World War, this was
the day where all community issues were solved and
discussed. Tables were set up and everyone shared food,
in addition to a lot of wine being drunk. Meschendorf
for example had six different *Nachbarschaften* each
having rules for different areas in the village. There
was a *Bruderschaft* that was lead by the *Altknecht*
and *Jungknecht* in addition to a *Schwesterschaft*.

On *Pfingsten* punishments would take place for acts
recorded throughout the year. For example it was
obligatory to go to church on Sundays, where one
had to be quiet within the church walls. If any of
these rules were broken they were recorded by the
Nachbarschaft and read out followed by punishments,
mainly fines, on *Pfingsten*. This once again questions the

Wedding Preparations (Pealing Potatoes). The entire community would help prepare for the Wedding.
Photograph: Meschendorf 1975

idea of voluntary and forced actions that took place
within Meschendorf and other Saxon villages. Was this
village really ideal, or was it just ideal in memory?

An agricultural festival was 'Peter and Paul's Day'
also known as the *Kronenfest*. The *Kronenfest* would
start in the early afternoon of the 29th of June.
Everyone in the village would dress in traditional
clothes, known as *'Tracht'* and would gather at the
Tanzplatz where the *Blaskapelle*, would play music.
Everyone would bring food and drinks to share. Benches
were constructed out of mud prior to the *Tanzplatz*
being built out of stone. A crown woven out of oak
leaves and flowers, which the village girls collected
and prepared two days prior to the festival, would
be raised on a massive wooden pole. The festival is
based on an agricultural tradition where the village
prays for prosperity, a bountiful harvest, overall
human well-being and a divine blessing. A young boy
would climb the pole up to the crown where he would
hold a speech asking for prosperity. The festival
shows the Saxons strong relationship to both the
Church, and agriculture, and brings great emphasis on
the importance agricultural success has on their well-
being and wealth.

> A Saxon woman recalls her memories of Peter and
> Paul's day. She describes how the youngsters
> made a *Trachtenumzug* and *Trachtenaufmarsch*
> (parade where they wore traditional clothing).
> Afterwards everyone began to dance. For this
> special occasion, she says that their mothers
> made the children *Baumstriezel* (a special
> confection)

The entire village took part in wedding celebrations.
Everyone worked together to prepare for the big day.
Weddings would cater for around 300 people. Quite
often marriages occurred within the same village,
only in the late 19th century was it more common to
marry someone from another Saxon town or village,
and only in recent years has it been acceptable
to marry a 'foreigner' someone who is not Saxon.[31]

31   "Popular Science Monthly/Volume 31/May 1887/Among the Transylvanian
Saxons I - Wikisource." Wikisource, the Free Library. Popular Science Monthly Volume
31 May 1887. Web. Aug. 2011. <http://en.wikisource.org/wiki/Popular_Science_Monthly/
Volume_31/May_1887/Among_the_Transylvanian_Saxons_I> p102

Saxon House Decorated for a Wedding
Photograph: Weisskirch 2011

Wedding preparation would start on Friday evening where everyone from the village (even those that were not invited) would donate drinks and foods such as livestock, eggs, potatoes, pigs, wines etc. On Saturday the butchering of the animals would take place, and the bread was baked. The *Gemeindesaal* community hall where the wedding celebrations took place was decorated. The entrance gates of the bride and grooms houses, (who still lived with their families) was decorated with pine tree branches and ornaments. The *Brautverziehung* would also take place on Saturday. The bride was hidden by her guests and the groom was challenged to find her, then the reverse would take place. Whoever found the other faster would be awarded with a gift such as wine. The wedding ceremony took place on Sundays, where the *Blaskapelle* would go to the groom's house with his guests. They would pick up the groom and go to the brides' house. At the brides house the groom had to lure her out of her families home and once again ask for her hand in marriage. After the brides' acceptance, everyone would go to church together. After the church ceremony the presents were left at the bride and grooms house. Everyone would meet at the *Gemeindesaal* which was filled with various different foods prepared by the entire village on the previous day. There would be *Tanzmusik* playing from around 2am until the early hours on Monday (often around 6 or 7 a.m.). Monday afternoon was known as *Resteessen*, which means eating the leftovers. Everyone would meet again in the *Gemeindesaal* and eat the leftover foods from the wedding. What was not eaten was then taken home. A Saxon could not let anything go to waste.

Christmas was also a 3-day communal celebration, where Christmas Eve, the most important day, was celebrated on the 24th of December. Wood was collected from everyone in the neighbourhood to create fires for heating and cooking. Children from the 5-8th grade would sing songs and recite poems before receiving a bag of gingerbread. Everyone would attend an evening mass before going home and having dinner with their family followed by Santa's visit sharing his gifts. The celebration often lasted until 8 am in the morning.

As one past resident recalls her memories on
Christmas she describes how on Christmas Eve
there would be a Christmas tree set up in the
Altaarraum of the church. The tree was decorated
with home backed cookies, apples bonbons,
straw stars and wax candles. Underneath the
tree, the children sang Christmas carols,
and recited poems (and nibbled on cookies
and candies from the Christmas tree). After
the ceremony, every child was given a heart
shaped gingerbread (which the mothers had
previously backed together in the *Pfarrhaus*),
in addition to other candies. Afterwards the
children were allowed to leave the altar
room through a 'side door', which lead to
the outside. The side door, she believes,
was only used by the children for Christmas
service. On all other occasions, she says
the door was only used by the priest.

She goes on to describe other events
within Meschendorf such as *St. Nikolaustag*
(celebration of St. Nicholas). She explains
how the children placed their shoes on the
windowsills where they recited poems. The
next morning the children's shoes were
filled with nuts, oranges, and candies.

On New Years she says that the children
visited their relatives and godparents to whom
they recited a New Years poem, wishing them a
happy New Year. In return the children were
thanked with nuts, oranges, candies and money.

In Meschendorf (and other villages in
Siebenbürgen) it was not the birthdays that
were celebrated, but the names days. It was
custom that all the children from the village
would visit the child the night before his
or her names day, and sang songs in front
of their door. In return the children were
invited into the families home where there
would be cake and lemonade to share. As a
present, the child who's names day it was,

Dance group with Maria Mueller at Dance competition in Reps
Photograph: Meschendorf 1958

would receive flowers (out of the garden of
the parents) and candies. On the names day
itself, the flowers would be placed onto the
windowsill, facing the street. This way
passers by always knew in which house names
day was being celebrated. The fact that the
flowers were placed on the windowsills shows
the Saxons need of public display. Whenever
they were proud of something they wanted to
show it. These are some of the memories the
Saxon woman remembered very well, and with a
lot of joy

The *Blaskapelle* still plays a major role in the
Meschendorfer Saxons life today. The band members
frequently gather for major events that take place.
Through this they are trying to uphold their tradition.
Although each member lives in a different area in
Germany they gather together to perform every four
years, at the Meschendorfer re-union in Germany. At
the re-union the Saxons re-enact various festivals
and traditions. The *Blaskapelle* also still plays at
many Meschendorfer Saxons funeral that takes place
within Germany (of which according to Mitz there were
around 50 deaths since the revolution). As previously
mentioned, they also played at Mitz's 100th birthday
showing how although they now live in separate areas,
they still unite for special occasions.

MITTELGASSE

The *Mittelgasse* is the main street in Meschendorf where most of the Saxon houses lie. In front of each home stands a bench, where a Saxon would sit in the evening to observe others in the very little spare time he had. It was very typical for a Saxon to watch their neighbour, and to be watched, to see if everything that is happening within the village is in its correct order.

Meschendorf appears to be an ideal society, but at the same time the community is very narrow and internal. The Saxon social order developed over the centuries, and established a system that secured a solid, organized community life. It also guaranteed that the German traditions, language, and virtues, were kept alive. It is this spirit that many emigrated Saxons remember when they recall their youth in an almost idyllic way. However, reality was more than only romantic life. It can almost be described as a community where people obey prescribed rules without questioning. If one of the rules are broken they are punished with public display, or forgotten in silence. A glimpse into the real life in Meschendorf is given in the novel *'Bis in das dritte und vierte Glied: Eine Familiengeschichte'* by Harald Von Hochmeister published in 2088. It tells the saga of a Meschendorf family where - just like on all human societies - greed, adultery and fraud were part of everyday life.

However, the social mechanism worked to maintain an efficient co-habitation. The Meschendorf Saxons were divided into seven different *Nachbarschaften,* who governed the village through a strict code of behaviour. The idea of the *Nachbarschaften* originated from the Saxons cultural links to the Mosel-Frankish idea of co-operative structures[32]. All boys belonged to the *Bruderschaft*, or brotherhood from confirmation until marriage, whereas all girls belonged to the *Schwesterschaft* sisterhood. This ordering system was so that all young people were controlled to certain conformity, and respected the rules of the village. Once a Saxon was married, he would become part of the

---

32   Ambrosi, Gerhard. "Carl Wolff and the Significance of Co-operative Ideas for the Regional Development of Transylvania." UNIVERSITY OF TRIER, 2002. Web. 3 Dec. 2011. <http://www.siebenbuerger.de/pdf/carl-wolff-ambrosi_englisch.pdf>. p 5

Nachbarschaft. This was reduced from seven to around three *Nachbarschaften* during the communist time. There were approximately 40 Saxons in every *Nachbarschaft,* and the *Nachbarvater* (leader of each group) was changed approximately every two years.

The purpose of the *Nachbarschaften* was to set rules, monitor the village, and assist in aid. A lot of work that took place in Meschendorf was undertaken by the entire community, ranging from wedding arrangements, to building a house. Each *Nachbarschaft* was symbolized through an engraved piece of wood, known as the *Nachbarschaftszeichen.* When anyone required assistance, for example to fix a roof, they would go to the Nachbarschaftsvater and ask for aid from the neighbourhood. The Nachbarschaftsvater would pass the Nachbarschaftszeichen to his neighbour telling him that he should help fix the roof on the following day, he would then pass the Nachbarschaftszeichen to the next neighbour, passing on the message, and so on, until the Nachbarschaftzeichen was returned to the Nachbarschaftsvater as a symbol that everyone received the message. The next day everyone would show up at the neighbour's house and aid with the reconstruction of the roof. Not only were tasks controlled by the Nachbarschaft but also daily rules of etiquette such as elbows on a table while eating, or slouching in church. If one failed to upkeep these rules, it was recorded and (often symbolic) punishment was made, as previously mentioned on *Pfingsten.*

Saxons had very strict rules about family life, and this included marriage. To solve marriage problems there was a church in the village of Biertan that also functioned as a 'couples prison'. The 'prison' was a single room that only contained one bed, one table, one chair, one plate, one glass and one set of cutlery. The couple having marriage problems was forced to stay in this room until all issues were resolved, and they were able to share and live together in harmony again. This shows how the Saxon family must always live in accord, even if their emotions towards each other were otherwise.

Saxon Church Gown from the early 1900's.
Photograph: Meschendorf 2011

Although this method of the 'couples prison' was not used in Meschendorf, it shows how the Saxons lived under a strict code where law and order was not an option but an obligation. It could almost be described as a society where personal choice did not play a major role in ones actions, but instead all actions and consequences were pre-decided.

Saxons also had set rules on the way they dressed showing their need of expressing their identity even on a visual basis. For centuries it was frowned upon not to wear traditional clothing, and the introduction of any 'foreign' clothes, such as Hungarian influence was banned. Only in the 19th century was it permitted to wear other clothing in towns, where the traditional clothing though still played a major role during ceremonies. In the villages though, the traditional Saxon dress continued to play a major role for a further 200 years. This was in an attempt to preserve a continuously shrinking minority group until the present day. It also showed how the Saxons like to be recognized as their own culture even in the way they dress.

While going through items left in my grandfather's old and fragile house, I come across two dresses and a church gown. I quickly changed into the dress to see myself as a Saxon in the mirror. The dresses did not have buttons but were fastened through ribbons and pins. Getting dressed was a long process leaving oneself in an upright position once everything had been fastened and tightened properly. The Saxons themselves often wove the fabrics. A large weaving frame still stands in my grandfather's home.

___FOOD

Saxon food was more piquant than foods found in Germany, as various recipes were borrowed from the Hungarian and Romanian cuisine. A very typical Saxon speciality is *Hanklich*, an in-between of bread and cake. It was made out of simple products; eggs, flower yeast, butter and milk, and baked flat in a tin. On special occasions

and festivities *Hanklich* was served with cream spread.
As a general rule, three meals were eaten daily.
Breakfast was eaten at 7 a.m. In the summer time, the
breakfast and lunch consisted of soup, mainly speck
and bread whereas in winter breakfast often consisted
of *Palukesbrei*, which was a type of corn porridge.
This was followed by a piece of fried sausage that was
cut using a tense string. To drink, the Saxons often
had milk, buttermilk and/or wine. Lunch was consumed
at mid-day. The most typical lunch was *Henkeltopf
Suppe* (soup) with speck, beans, cabbage and onions,
in addition to drinking water. The soup for lunch was
taken out onto the fields in a sealed *Henkeltopf*, where
it was placed in the sun to be warmed by mid-day.
On grey days, the pot was wrapped in various cloths
to keep it warm, or the soup was eaten cold. Around
six people on the fields shared one soup pot. Martin
describes how from the fields one could always tell
that it was mid-day due to the way the shadow from the
church fell onto the village ground. At around 5 p.m.
it was time for *Brotzeit,* which translated means time
for bread. To no surprise, this is exactly what was
consumed at this time of day, small cold meats with
bread. In the evening *Palukes* (the local name for corn)
was served with cheese and sausage. Unlike the more
liquid *Palukes* Saxons had for breakfast, it was fried
into small disks, which made it almost bread like. The
cheese was then placed between two *Palukes*.

The daily routine of the villages is still
controlled by the milking of the cows. During
my visit in Meschendorf I was woken up daily at
6am by the sounds of cows passing outside the
windows. After milking, the cowherd led the
cows through the main street in Meschendorf
from the *Scheune* every morning, out onto
the hills where they would graze. In the
evening the cows returned to their stable,
by themselves, knowing the way to the farm
gate. This is a daily routine that can still
be seen today, and was common throughout the
years.

Saxons highly enjoyed their different thick soups. One very typical soup was a bean soup in bread. The bread was cut at one end, and carved out in the inside, turning the bread into a hollow and functioning edible bowl. Other typical thicker soups were the *Saure Bauern Suppe* (sour farmers soup), Sauerkraut Suppe (sauerkraut soup), *Speck and Knoedel Suppe* (speck and dumpling soup), and Kartoffel Suppe (potato soup).

If a Saxon was lucky enough to own or even distil his own *Schnaps* he would take a sip in the morning and evening to "strengthen his health". Wine was only owned by very few, in addition to cigarettes, due to the poverty of most Saxons. Cigarettes were also not a necessity for the Saxons, and therefore didn't appeal to their stingy nature. This is also why very few men smoked, and if they did, this would only occur on Sundays. For a woman to smoke would have been unacceptable. This shows how the Saxon society was very male dominated and structured to certain rules and etiquettes.

Previous Page:
Romanian Orthodox Church
Photograph: Meschendorf 2011

UNTERGASSE

___THE ROMANIAN ORTHODOX CHURCH

At the lower part of the village, where the *Mittelgasse* meets the *Untergasse* is the Romanian Orthodox Church, which marks the growing population of Romanians and Romas within the Saxon villages. The church is well maintained and surrounded by Saxon houses that have been marked by Romanians, which inhabit them, through the cross underneath the Dutch gable.

Romanians have always lived in minorities on the border of Saxon villages, but now make up the majority of most Saxon villages including Meschendorf. There has always been segregation between Romanians and other nationalities in Romania including the Saxons. This form of 'differentiation' could already be seen in the 13th century, when all of Transylvania was an autonomous principality under the Hungarian crown, as most noble men were Hungarian but the peasants were often Romanian. There was also a strong segregation in Meschendorf between the Romanians and Saxons, which can still be seen today. The Saxons lived in bigger, well-maintained houses on the *Obergasse* and *Mittelgasse* whereas the few Romanian residents lived on the *Untergasse* in smaller homes. The Romanians would not take part in festivities and cultural events. They were the poorer group, often serving as street cleaners, or herdsmen in the fields for the Saxon farmers. Nevertheless the Romanians and Romas were treated better under Saxon rule, than anywhere else in Romania. Even today, Romanians remain very poor compared to other citizens in their country and often turn to working in the construction and service industry in countries such as Greece, Spain and Italy as they make more money than university professors or engineers make back home in Romania.

Romanians started to live in Meschendorf in the late 1940's after the end of World War II. It is said by various Meschendorfer Saxons that a Romanian man spread the word to various Romanian families that

Romas in local 'Pub' in Meschendorf
Photograph: Meschendorf 2011

the Saxons have left their houses, land and lively
stock behind, which now required someone to take over.
Soon later, around 80 Romanian families arrived in
Meschendorf, only to find that this had been untrue,
and that most Saxons still remained in their homes
in Meschendorf. A man called Roman, who was a self
nominated mayor from the communist party arrived with
a *Namensbuch* (book with names) stating the rites of
the Romanian families to live in the Saxon houses.
The Saxons were not evicted from their homes, but
instead were obliged to share their homes with the
newly arrived Romanian families. After around two
days, it is said that a lot of Romanian families left
after realising that living together like this was
not possible, and that the rumour of available, empty
Saxon homes had been a political hoax. Nevertheless
around 20 Romanian families remained in Meschendorf
who then built their own homes in the lower part of
Meschendorf from money funded by the state in 1956.

Over the last 20 years, many Saxons adopted a
pragmatic approach and invited, Romanian families,
with farming ambitions, to rent or even buy their
homes so that they are maintained in their absence.
Nevertheless, some Saxons are still hesitant about
seeing their heritage disappear. While most Saxons
would agree that a Romanian farmer works as hard as
a Saxon, there is still a sense of prejudice between
the two cultures and Romanians are often seen as
thieves. During my stay in Meschendorf I heard subtle
allegations that the Romanians and Romas are known
for steeling within the village. The worst theft in
Meschendorf appears to be the disappearing organ pipes
of the Lutheran church. It is suspected that the pipes
were sold, so that the metal could be melted to produce
other goods. There is even the bizarre story that
the local police station was robbed and the police
car stolen-anecdotes that tell that stereotypical
descriptions of ethnical behavior are still prevalent.

When the Romanians are questioned regarding
stealing, they point the blame onto the Romas, and
state their concern that Romas soon will outnumber

Farmer reuturning to his home on horse carriage, the main form of transport used by Meschendorf residents.
Photograph: Meschendorf 2011

them in the Saxon villages. The Meschendorf Romas often work for the Romanian farmers on irregular basis, as unemployed among Romas is very high. The local shop in the *Untergasse* also functions as a small pub, where the Romas hang out from morning to dawn with a bottle of beer – a scene that confirm the prejudice for many who return for a visit to re-imagine old times.

Romania has now been part of the EU since 2007[33]. This has had a great affect on how Romanian citizens are able to live and work within their country. Some of the benefits that came out of joining the EU were that various roads were repaired, utilities became more reliable, and economic reform was implemented. Nevertheless inevitably, problems also occurred such as inflation and an ill-considered ban on horse carts on fast roads, which many farmers relied on for transportation. The EU membership also endangered free roaming of cow and sheep herds, the ability to sell unpasteurised cheese on roadsides, in addition to strict and unforeseeable regulations on slaughtering farm animals, which resulted in jeopardising livelihoods of many Romanians who rely on the farming industry.

Therefore it is inevitable, that even if the Romanians wished to work as hard as the Saxons used to, and set up their own farms in the same way the Saxons used to, they wouldn't be allowed by law. In the same way, if the Saxons had not left, their life too would have changed, as they would not be able to maintain their past customs and way of life, as farming and agriculture now has restrictions where free roaming, or slaughtering of animals is not permitted without licensing, two factors which played a major role in the Saxons daily life.

As Helmuth, reflects, "Recalling my childhood memories of Meschendorf, I remember a life in a village that was vibrant and full of things to do. We were always a group of German kids playing together (Romanians, and Gypsy children tended to stay at the outer-skirts of the village, as their families lived there). Our favourite games were of course football or cowboys. The

33   Pettersen, Leif. Baker, Mark. 'Romania'.(Lonely Planet 2010)p 37

winter always brought a lot of snow, allowing us to use our sleighs from the church all the way down the main street, until the bridge. The lake was also always frozen; allowing us to use self-improvised hockey sticks, simple ice-skates (mostly these were just metal pieces attached to the shoes with wires) to play ice hockey from sunrise to sunset. I must also mention the fact that it was necessary to find a tin as hockey puck.

On cold evenings we often got ourselves some wine from the cellars, without the awareness of our parents of course, to make some nice warm *Gluehwein* (mulled-wine). At some stage we became specialists at making *Gluehwein*, and this already at the tender age of 12-13 years. Of course we never got drunk, but we were definitely merry.

I can of course also remember all the green pastures and meadows on which the cows were grazing. My brother and I were often allowed to accompany our grandfather and his skilled dogs. My grandfather was in charge of a special species of cows (a couple hundred of them), they were known as Hereford, and were imported from America. They were purely cultured for their meat. I remember having an amazing time on these fields, especially as the dogs listened to our every command, circling around the herds of cows making sure that they were all kept together.

I could spend hours just recalling various memories of the past. For example, at the age of around 9 my brother and I started to learn how to play instruments. After around 2-3 years of practice we were already playing in the *Seniorenblaskapelle* rather than the *Jugendblaskapelle* of which we were very proud. Another climax was also the Confirmation process, which was of high importance in Saxon tradition. After Confirmation took place, you were recognised as being a teenager, which meant that you were allowed to attend every *Tanzball* (dance), which always took place until 6am."

Photograph: Meschendorf 2011

More than 700 years of Saxon history are slowly disappearing. The Saxon culture, as the emigrated Saxons remember, was an autonomous identity that survived many attacks over the centuries. The Saxons were ruled by a regulated community, with a strict code of conduct, which is also reflected within their architecture; as seen with the communal food storage within the church, the *Tanzplatz* as their central gathering point for events, and the Saxon home that housed various generations of one family in a single space. The German villages have long been dissolved with Meschendorf only being one example of this. The memories that Saxons contemplate when visiting their place of birth are idealized, nostalgic memories of a close-knit community. It is important to note and document the rich Saxon culture that has survived though various generations for over 700 years, especially as these customs are being lost and forgotten through their absence, and the new Romania and Roma families moving in. Nevertheless it is also important to remember that most of the Saxon stories show Meschendorf in an ideal light, as it is no more a village that exists in the same way, but a village kept in Memory.

The main obstacles that resulted in the Saxons leaving Meschendorf have been resolved, and yet no Saxon returned. Romania has adopted a democratic system and in 2005 the property restitution law, to reclaim ones buildings, which were held in communism time, was introduced. The Saxons adapted, and now enjoy the more economically developed countries they have settled in. Meschendorf is now no more than a temporary location where Saxons visit their home to reflect, and contemplate on past memories, of a village that will never exist the same way as it used to. Indeed, it is a common aspect that occurred throughout Europe, especially due to new strict rules on the rural way of life. But it is also due to an additional hardship the village has undergone through political reasons.

As Helmuth, my Grandfather's nephew said: "The village is literally dead. What's left is the backdrop of a stage, crumbling, and only kept up by repairs done by the former inhabitants that want to keep their memory intact."

The mass emigration phenomenon has had extreme consequences on the rural areas and landscape, leaving hundreds of villages, including Meschendorf deserted. Romanians, and predominately Romas, who brought with them a new culture, religion and working ethic, have now inhabited some villages. Previously, the Saxons were "self sufficient" both in agriculture and economy and had a great sense of cooperation within their own communities and surrounding neighbourhoods. The Romanians, and mainly Romas though, lack this sense of community and skill, to maintain themselves, which has resulted in both poverty and dereliction in addition to new laws not allowing for free farming, the main industry Meschendorf relied on.

"Remembering last summer's visit to Meschendorf, I recall an internal feeling of sadness," recalls Helmuth. With the emigration of the Saxons the entire face and infrastructure of the village has changed. Various houses are broken, or are on the verge of falling apart. Many residents, mainly Romas, hang around in their houses or streets rather than cultivating the rich, fruitful soils. Of course there are also some wealthy Romanian families living in Meschendorf, but their children often leave for the cities to attend schools, learn a professions, and then settle in larger towns.

As the remaining Saxons say, "As long as our parents and relatives return to Meschendorf for visits, or summer holidays, as long as there are still people that are prepared to restore the church and take care of the maintenance of the graveyards, during this time, the spirit of the Saxons in Meschendorf will remain." The question is though, what will happen when this generation dies? There are not many newcomers in Meschendorf, apart from the few that are re-buying their homes as a summerhouse for vacations.

BIBLIOGRAPHY

Books

Foisel, John. 'Saxons through the Seventeen Centuries: A history of the Transyvanian Saxons'. (Cleveland, Ohio. Central Alliance of Transylvanian Saxons in the United States, 1936.)

Hannover, Brigitta G. 'Rumaenien entdecken: Kunstschaetze und Naturschoenheiten'. (Berlin. Trescher-Reihe Reisen, 2007).

John M. Cabot's "The Racial Conflict in Transylvania" The Beacon Press; 1St Edition edition (1926)

Manea, Norman. 'The Hoolidan's Return: A memoir'. (New York. Farrar, Straus and Giroux 2003.)

Mueller, Herta. 'Niederung'. (Muenchen. Carl Hanser, 2010)

Pettersen, Leif. Baker, Mark. 'Romania'.(Lonely Planet 2010)

Riley, Bronwen. 'Transylvania'. (London. Frances Lincoln Limited, 2007.)

Sebald, W.G. 'Die Ausgewanderten: Vierl lange Erzaehlungen'. (Frankfurt am Main. Fischer Taschenbuch Verlag, 2009)

Toepfer, Friedrich. 'Meschendorf am Steinberg'. (Nuernberg. Siebenbuergrisch-Sachsische Stiftung, 2000)

Von Hochmeister, Harald. 'Bis in das dritte und vierte Glied: Eine Familiengeschichte'. (Sibiu. Editura Universitatii "Lucian Blaga", 2008.)

Articles

Cercel, C. "The relationship between religious and national identity in the case of Transylvanian Saxons (1933-1944)" Nationalities papers. Vol 39, No. 2. 2011: 161-180

Davis, S. E. "Maintaining a "German" home in Southeast Europe: Transylvanian Saxon nationalism and the metropolitan model of the family, 1918-1933" . The history of the family : an international quarterly. Vol 14. No. 4. 2009: 386-401

De Tregomain, P. "Constructing Authenticity: Commemorative Strategy of the Transylvanian Saxons in West Germany's Early Years" Ostfildern; Thorbecke. 2006

Georgescu, T. 'Ethnic minorities and the eugenic promise: the Transylvanian Saxon experiment with national renewal in inter-war Romania'. European review of history. Vol. 17. No. 6. 2010: 861-880¬

Koranyi, J. Wittlinger, R. "From Diaspora to Diaspora: The Case of Transylvanian Saxons in Romania and Germany" Nationalism & ethnic politics. Vol 17, no. 1. 2011: 96-115.

Internet

Ambrosi, Gerhard. "Carl Wolff and the Significance of Co-operative Ideas for the Regional Development of Transylvania." UNIVERSITY OF TRIER, 2002. Web. 3 Dec. 2011. <http://www.siebenbuerger.de/pdf/carl-wolff-ambrosi_englisch.pdf>.

Antoni, Hermine. "Treffen in Meschendorf." Meschendorfer Homepage. H.O.G. Web. 1 Nov. 2011. http://www.meschendorf7bgn.de/

"Building Sustainably by Learning from Traditional Architecture." INTBAU - International Network for Traditional Building, Architecture & Urbanism. Web. Sep. 2011. <http://www.intbau.org/archive/courses.htm>.

"ENCYCLOPAEDIA BRITANNICA." Corvinus Library - Hungarian History. Web. Nov. 2011. <http://www.hungarianhistory.com/lib/faf/toc06.htm>.

Junesch, Herman. "Das Nachbarschaftswesen in Siebenbürgen." Homepage Tartlau. Tartlauer Nachbarschaft, 2009. Web. 3 Sept. 2011. <http://www.tartlau.eu/drupal/Nachbarschaft/Das-Nachbarschaftswesen-Siebenbuergen>.

"Meschendorf in Siebenbürgen." Aktion Pro Meschendorf. Web. 11 July 2011. http://meschendorf.ch/

"Popular Science Monthly/Volume 31/May 1887/Among the Transylvanian Saxons I - Wikisource." Wikisource, the Free Library. Popular Science Monthly Volume 31 May 1887. Web. Aug. 2011.

"Siebenbürger Sachsen." Wikipedia, the Free Encyclopedia. Web. 7 July 2011 http://de.wikipedia.org/wiki/Siebenbürger_ Sachsen

Stollberg, Robert, and Thomas Schulz. Kirchenburgen in Sie-benbürgen: Fortified Churches in Transylvania. Koeln: Boehlau, 2007. Web. 6 Oct. 2011. http://books.google.co.uk/books?id=mn CrJgK7OUwC&pg=PA16&lpg=PA16&dq=siebenbuerger+nachba rschaft+zeichen&source=bl&ots=HfNQK-w7TE&sig=JIDg4linNr-n7B7Lmuy4BrLU9C4&hl=en&sa=X&ei=Q1v3TqitBMaO8gPKn 9XKAQ&redir_esc=y#v=onepage&q=siebenbuerger%20nach-barschaft%20zeichen&f=false

"Transylvania." Wikipedia, the Free Encyclopedia. 15 Dec. 2011. Web. 3 Dec. 2011. <http://en.wikipedia.org/wiki/Transylvania>.

"The Saxon Villages of Transylvania, Romania. A future for the Mediaeval Landscape." Kim Wilkie Assoiates. Nov. 2001. Web 11 Sep. 2011. http://www.kimwilkie.com/images/projects/ovs/ transylv/transylvania_prt1.pdf

"The Vanished Romanian German Community Through Hitler's Population Transfer, Soviet Deportation, & Mass Emigration." In-stitute for Research of Expelled Germans. Web. 22 Sept. 2011. <http://expelledgermans.org/transylvaniasaxons.htm>.

"Whole Village Projects Mesendorf-Meschendorf -Mese." The Mihai Eminescu Trust. 2002. Web. Sept. 2011. <http://www. mihaieminescutrust.org/content/nd_village.asp?n=97>.

Images

Seivert, J. Das hohe Lied Salomos in Siebenburgischsachsischer Sprache. London. Privately Printed for Pince Louis Lucien
Bonaparte, 1859.

"Pied Piper". http://4.bp.blogspot.com/_loU3bEFUwWc/TCX_
C9PRKtl/AAAAAAAAJJI/HEnPxzQoJrQ/s1600/Pied+Piper.jpg

"Saxon Fortified Churches in Siebenbuergen" (Toepfer,
Friedrich. P. 2)

"Who died in war" (Toepfer, Friedrich. P. 78)

"Wedding preperation" (Toepfer, Friedrich. P. 108)

"Interior of Church" (Toepfer, Friedrich. P. 130)

"Elementary school report" (Toepfer, Friedrich. P. 236)

"Das Stufenalter Des Mannes"

http://shop.billerantik.de/products/Baeuerliches/Bilder/Stufenal-
ter-des-Mannes-Geburt-Ehe-Tod-Lebensrad-BBB-7.html

"Map of Schafsburger, Herrmanstadtler, Repser region villages
in Transylvania"
"File:Josephinische Landaufnahme Pg208.jpg." Wikipedia, the
Free Encyclopedia. Web. Sept. 2011. <http://en.wikipedia.org/
wiki/File:Josephinische_Landaufnahme_pg208.jpg>.

"The dissolution of Austria-Hungary"
"File:AustriaHungaryWWI.gif." Wikipedia, the Free Ency-
clopedia. Web. Sept. 2011. <http://en.wikipedia.org/wiki/
File:AustriaHungaryWWI.gif>

"Goldene Freibrief Andreas II from 1224 through King Karl I.
"File:Goldener Freibrief 1224.jpg." Wikipedia, the Free
Encyclopedia. Web. Nov. 2011. <http://en.wikipedia.org/wiki/
File:Goldener_freibrief_1224.jpg>

"Meschendorf showing the Saxon Lutheran Church at the top
of the Mittelgasse..."
http://static2.tripwolf.com/raw/showmedia/thumb/63103/460

All photographs taken 1980 by Ruth Klein

All photographs taken 2011 by Jessica Klein

APPENDIX

INTERVIEWS

Meschendorf Sieberbürger Saxons

Ich bitte um Ihre Unterstützung für einen Bericht über Meschendorf

Mein Name ist Jessica Klein. Mein Großvater Georg Klein ist in Meschendorf
aufgewachsen, und vielleicht können Sie sich sogar an ihn erinnern. Ich lebe
mit meiner Familie in London, mein Vater heisst Roland Klein. Als Enkelin
von Georg Klein habe Ich grosses Interesse an der Geschichte Siebenbürgens
und besonders Meschendorf. Das hat mich dazu bewegt, meine Abschlussarbeit
im Rahmen meines Architekturstudiums über Meschendorf zu schreiben. Ich
bitte Sie dafür um Ihre Unterstützung. Würden Sie mir bitte einige Fragen
beantworten die ich gerne - anonym - in meine Arbeit einfliessen lassen will.
Ich schreibe meine Arbeit über die vergangen Traditionen, Architektur, und
Lebensweise im Vergleich zu heute. Ich wäre Ihnen sehr dankbar wenn Sie mir
Antworten liefern könnten, auch wenn sie nur einige Fragen betrifft. Ich bin
für jede Information dankbar.

1.   Name:

2.   Alter:

3.   Bis wann haben Sie in Meschendorf gelebt?

4.   Wie oft haben Sie Meschendorf seit Ihrer Auswanderung besucht? Was
waren die drei größten Eindrücke? (Veränderungen kulturell, Architektur usw)

5.   Sie sind per Geburt Siebenbürger Sachse? Was definiert einen Siebenbürger Sachsen? (Falls Sie in Deutschland geboren sind: welche Antwort würden
Sie geben?)

6.   Gehört ihnen noch ein Haus/Grundstück in Meschendorf

7.   Schliesslich: Wenn sie noch weitere Information über Meschendorfer Architektur, Traditionen und Tägliches Leben ergänzen wollen - bitte schildern
Sie es hier. Ich bin für jede Auskunft dankbar..

Vielen Dank für ihre freundliche Unterstützung.

Beste Grüße

Jessica Klein

I would like to ask for your help in answering these questions for my dissertation about Meschendorf.

My name is Jessica klein. My grandfather is Georg Klein, who grew up in Meschendorf. Possibly you may even remember him. I currently live in London
with my family, and father, Roland Klein. I have great interest in the history of Siebenbürgen, especially Meschendorf. This inspired me to write my
dissertation on Meschendorf. I would really appreciate your help, by answering the following questions. You can remain anonymous. I am writing about the
passt traditions, architecture and customs of the Transylvanian Saxons in
Meschendorf, and also comparing it to today. I am grateful for any information you could provide me with.

1. Name

2. Age

3. Until which date did you live in Meschendorf?

4. Since you emigrated from Meschendorf, how often have you visited Meschendorf? What were your three greatest impressions? (changes in culture, architecture etc)

5. Are you Siebenbürger Saxon from birth? What defines a Siebenbürger Saxon?
(incase you were born in Germany are you Saxon or German?)

6. Do you still own property in Meschendorf?

7. If you have any further information on Meschendorf please let me know. I
am grateful for any information and thoughts.

Thank you very much for your help an support,

best wishes

Jessica Klein

Frage 1+2   Martin Klein geb. 6.5.39 u Frieda
             geborene Binder 11.8.36 in Mexendorf

Frage 3   Vor dem 2 Weltkrieg hat keiner von der
             Deutschen minderheit   an das Aus
             wandren gedacht. Nach der Krieg waren
             die Familien zerstreut. Die noch über lebenden von der Siebenbürgersachsen durften nicht
             nachrese kommen nach Rumänien. Denn
             nach Kriegs ende wurden, alle Deutschstämige
             Frauen u Männer die noch arbeitsfähig
             waren nach Russland verschlept. Also
             der Rumänische Staat mußte Arbeit
             für den Russen leisten. So hat der
             Rumäne alle Deutsche minderheit
             hin gezwungen auf Arbeit. Dann
             die jenigen die in Russland Arbeits
             unfäg wurden durften ebenfals
             nicht Nachause, sondren wurden nach
             Deutschland ab geschoben. u das waren
             nicht wenige. So kam, das die Familien
             zerissen wurden. (Kinder u Mütter nicht zu
             den Vätern, Mütter nicht zu den Kindren)
             Die Mutter von meinem Schwager wurde
             Invaliede in Russland u dan abgeschoben
             nach Deutschland. Die Kinder kammen
             zur Mutter 1365. Im Jahre 1963 heiratete
             meine Schwester einen von den Brüdern, Die
             kamen dann zu ihrem Vater u Mann. Meine
             Mutter kam 1969 zu ihrer Tochter

Martin K. Born 6.5.39
and Frida B. born 11.8.36 in Meschendorf.

Before WWII no German minority group (in Transylvania) thought about emigrating. After the war many families were separated. The remaining Siebenbuerger
Saxons were not allowed to return to Romania. Then after the end of the war
the remaining people (with German heritage), who were still able to work,
were sent to Russia. The Romanian state had to give people that were able
to work to Russia. Those that were sent to Russia were also not allowed to
return home (to Transylvania), but were then sent to Germany (and these were
many). Through this many families were destroyed (Children and mothers were
not allowed to go to their fathers, and also Mothers not to their children.
The mother of my brother-in-law was sent to Russia, and then sent to Germany.
The children only returned to their mother in 1965. My mother came to her
daughter in 1969...

Im Jahre 1975 kam uns auch der
Gedanke auszureisen, die Hofenung
bestand ja. Anfang 60er Jahre
gab es ein Abkommen zwischen
Rumänien u Deutschland das sollte
Familien zusamenführung heisen.
(Aber es war alles andre) Der Gedanke
aus diesem Grund, es wurde für die
Deutsche bevölkerung immer sült-
barer das du als Minderheit an
gesehen warst. zb in guten Schulen
war es Schwieriger einen Platz zu kriegen.
            Einen guten Arbeitsplatz
zu bekomen mußtes du doppelt so
gut sein wie der Rumäne ssw.
            Im Jahr 1982 hatten wir unter
Schwirigen umständen die Ausreisegeneh-
migung erhalten. In den 12 Jahren
bis zur Ausreise war ich fast
jedes Jahr Wode 2x Beim Passamt
bei Partei u allen Ämtern wo man
sich beschweren konnte. Wir Aus
reise waligen trafen uns immer
Wieder die selben bei den Ämtren.
Wir wurden Verscheucht u bedroht von
irgend einigen zuständigen Herrn
(Werkzeug der Partei) u.s.w. Bis zu dieser
Zeit siend einzele Familie ausgesiedet
Nach der Mauerfal 1989 sind fast alle
Dörfer leer geworden.

130

...In 1975 we also thought about emigrating. The hope was there. In the
beginning of the 1960's there was an agreement between Romania and Germany
which should help bring families back together (but it was all different).
The problem: It was always hard to be seen as a minority. For example: It was
very hard to find a place in a good school, you would not get a good position
at work. To gain good work you had to be twice as good as the Romanian.

    In 1982 we received the permission to emigrate (after various
complications). In the 12 years before we emigrated I went to the border
control 1 or 2 times. Us, wishing to emigrate were always sent away. Various
families though managed to emigrate. After the fall of the Wall in 1989
almost all the Saxon villages became empty. ...

Fage 4

Im ersten Jahr nach de Aus-
raise durften Wir nicht instand
gelassen, ab dann waren wir fast
jedes Jahr in Siebenbürgen Rum.
Bis zum zusammenbruch
des Kommunismus musten Wir für
jeden Tag pro Person 25 DM um taus
en, so war das für meie Famili
3-4 Wochen viel Geld.
Verendet hat alles Felder kaum noch
bearbeitet, keine Unterhaltungen von
Jugedlichen mit Deutschen Lieder, Ville
zusamen Gebrochene Bauten,
verwüstete Höfe us.w.

Fage 5,

Ein Siebenbürgersachse ist geprägt wo
seit vor 800 Jaren da die ersten
Auswanderer von Deutschland nach
Siebenbürgen kamen, immer schwere
Schicksale zu meistern. (Da muste man eine
kleine Geschichte kennen, dis zum ausdru
zum bringen)
Ein Siebenbürgersachse hat die Schwirig
überwunden mit Respekt dem andren
gegenüber u mit eiserster Diszieplin,
sträng mit sich selbst, mit Geschick
lichkeit u viel, viell Fleiß u Gehorsamke

In the first year of having emigrated from Romania to Germany we were not allowed to return. After that year, we returned to Meschendorf, and other areas in Siebenbuergen, annually.

Until the fall of communism we had to pay 25 DM (in exchange) per day per person to be in Romania. Therefore it was very expensive to spend 3-4 weeks in Romania with your family.

Everything has changed, the fields are hardly being worked on, there is are no more entertainment (festivals) with young people singing German songs. There are a lot of collapsing buildings etc.

A Siebenbuerger Saxon carries a heavy burden since they arrived 800 years ago from Germany to Romania, as they carry with them difficult fates.

A Siebenbuerger Saxon has overcome difficult times with respect towards other people, and with the best discipline. He is strict with himself, has a lot of skills, diligence and obedience.

Liebe Jessica,   8/9/11

gerne erfülle ich dir deinen Wunsch. Dass ist ja eine ganz tolle Idee, über
Meschendorf die Abschlussarbeit zu schreiben.

Mein Name ist Anneliese B. geb. Orendt, 56 Jahre alt. Bin mit 23 Jahren aus
Meschendorf ohne meine Eltern wegen der Liebe ausgereist. In den ersten
Jahren bin ich 1- 2 mal in Jahr dahin gefahren weil meine Eltern und
Geschwister noch dort gelebt haben.

Seit 20 Jahren fahre ich regelmäßig alle zwei Jahre, im Sommer mit einer
Gruppe von Jugendlichen aus Berlin nach Rumänien und nach Meschendorf und
die sind alle sehr erstaunt, interessiert und begeistert.

Sehr berührt hat uns die Geburtstagsfeier vom Herrn Martin, dem 100 Jährigen
letztes Jahr den wir mit einem Geburtstagslied überrascht haben.

Was uns immer wieder sehr wundert ist, dass die Kirchenburg und die Kirche,
der Friedhof und das Pfarrgebäude saniert und gepflegt wird und es sogar
finanziell gefördert wird.

Was mich traurig stimmt ist, dass es kaum Menschen auf der Straße gibt, das
Leben hat sich sehr geändert und ich kenne die Menschen gar nicht die in den
Häusern wohnen. Einige Häuser sehen auch sehr verfallen aus. Doch wiederum
hat sogar Prinz Charles dieses kleine, versteckte, idylische Dorf gefunden.
Schade nur dass sein Mitwirken in der Öko Landwirtschaft aufhört, wenn ich
da richtig informiert bin.

In Bezug auf Umweltbewusstsein muss und sollte sich dort noch einiges
entwickeln lassen.

Ich und meine Eltern besitzen kein Grundstück mehr privat in Meschendorf.
Wir haben unser Haus und den Hof dort je nach Bedarf für soziale Projekte
zur Verfügung gestellt.

Zur Zeit bietet es einige Übernachtungsplätze. Es ist die Hausnummer 40.

Ich wünsche Ihnen weiter hin viel Spaß beim Entdecken und beim Sammeln von
Informationen über Meschendorf und viel Erfolg bei der Abschlussarbeit.

Ich habe auch ein großes Interesse daran ihre Arbeit zu lesen, wenn dass
möglich ist. DANKE !

Liebe Grüße aus Berlin

Anneliese B.
134

Dear Jessica,   8/9/11

I will answer your questions with pleasure. That is a great idea that you are writing about Meschendorf for your dissertation.

My name is Anneliese B.. I was born in Orendt, and am 56 years old. I left Meschendorf at the age of 23 for love and immigrated to Germany. During the first couple years I visited Meschendorf 1-2 times a year as my parents and siblings still lived there. Since the past 20 years I visit Meschendorf regularly, once every two years, with a group of teenagers from Berlin, that are surprised, astonished, and interested in Meschendorf upon their visit. It was also very touching to attend Herr Martin Werners birthday last year, whom we surprised with a birthday song for his 100 year celebration.

What always surprises us is that the Fortified church, graveyard and the Pfarrgebaeude is always maintained and even gains financial aid.

What makes me really sad is that there are no more people on the streets. The life there changed a lot, and I do not even know the people that live in the houses there anymore. A lot of the houses also look as though they are falling apart. Then again, even Prince Charles has found this hidden idyllic village. Unfortunately though he has terminated his aid for the development of the Organic farm, if I am informed correctly. In relation to the awareness of the environment, I feel that there still have to be many more changes done in Meschendorf.

My parents and I do not own land or a house in Meschendorf anymore. We have given our house and farm for the availability of social projects. Currently it offers some spaces to sleep in. It is the number 40.

I wish you the best of luck and joy with the collection of information on Meschendorf. I also have a great interest in reading your dissertation once it is completed, if this is possible. THANK YOU!

Best wishes from Berlin

Anneliese B.

8/9/11

Name: Folberth R.

Alter: 36, habe bis zu meinen 15 Lebensjahr in Meschendorf gelebt.

Fahre 3 bis 4 mal im Jahr nach Meschendorf, ich besitze da noch zwei Häuser.

Schöne Grüße aus Sachsen b. Ansbach

Rolf F.

                                                     Meschendorf Sieberbürger Saxons
Name: Folberth R.

Age: 36 years. Lived in Meschendorf until the age of 15.

Drive 3 to 4 times per year to Meschendorf, I still own two houses there.

Best wishes from Sachsen b. Ansbach

Rold F.

12/9/11

1. Name: Thomas K.

2. Alter: 22

3. Bis wann haben Sie in Meschendorf gelebt? gar nicht

4. Wie oft haben Sie Meschendorf seit Ihrer Auswanderung besucht? Was waren
die drei größten Eindrücke? (Veränderungen kulturell, Architektur usw)

Fünf mal war ich bereits da, und ich liebe die ruhige Belassenheit der Natur
sowie der Architektur. Es gleicht einer Zeitreise in ein längst vergangenes
Jahrhundert.

5. Sie sind per Geburt Siebenbürger Sachse. Was definiert einen Siebenbürger
Sachsen? (Falls Sie in Deutschland geboren sind: welche Antwort würden Sie
geben?)

Ich bin Stolz auf die mir mitgegebene Kultur, und trotzdessen das ich in
Deutschland geboren wurde, habe ich eine starke Heimatverbundenheit zu Siebenbürgen.

In meinem Freundeskreis sind div. siebenbürger Sachsen und es ist eine andere
Gesellschaft, andere Werte und ein Zusammengehörigkeitsgefühl

6. Gehört ihnen noch ein Haus/Grundstueck in Meschendorf? nein, aber meine
Familie

1. Name: Thomas K.

2. Age: 22

3. Until which date did you live in Meschendorf? never

4. Since you emigrated from Meschendorf, how often have you visited Meschendorf? What were your three greatest impressions? (changes in culture, architecture etc)

I have been to Meschendorf five times. I love the quietness of the surrounding nature and architecture. It is like experiencing a time travel into a bygone century.

5. Are you Siebenbürger Saxon from birth? What defines a Siebenbürger Saxon? (incase you were born in Germany are you Saxon or German?)

I am proud of the (Saxon) culture given to me, and although I was born in Germany I feel strong ties to Siebenbuergen, Transylvania.
   In my group of friends (in Germany) there are also Siebenbuerger Saxons, it is a different community, with other values and sense of community.

6. Do you still own property in Meschendorf? No, but my family do. They have not gained it all back yet tho.

9/9/11

Frage 1: Arthur Simon

Frage 2: 28 Jahre

Frage 3: 1989

Frage 4: Jedes Jahr seit 1989

Frage 5: Stolz, für unsere Kultur

Frage 7: ja

Mit freundlichen Grüßen

Arthur S.

Question 1: Arthur Simon

Question 2: 28 years

Question 3: 1989

Question 4: Every year since 1989

Question 5: Proud, of our culture

Question 7: yes

With friendly wishes

Arthur S.

11/9/11

Guten Tag

Eine kleine Unterstützung für dein Vorhaben.

1.) mein Name ist Konradt G.

2.) Ich bin 52 Jahre alt

3.) Ich habe in Meschendorf bis zu meinem 17 Lebensjahr (1976) gelebt

4.) Wir haben Meschendorf 7 mal besucht, und jedes Mal ist uns bewusst geworden dass es fast aus gestorben und verlassen ist.

Die alten Häuser sind dem Verfall überlassen.

Da fast keine Leute mehr in Meschendorf sind, werden die alte Bräuche nicht mehr gehalten und weitergeleitet.

5.) Diese Frage ist nicht leicht zu beantworten: Ehrlichkeit und Fleiß, ein Mensch der es wagt einen Neuanfang.

6.) Nein ich habe kein eignes Haus in Meschendorf, nur mein Elternhaus, um das kümmert sich mein Bruder.

Hoffentlich konnte ich dir mit meinen kurzen Antworten weiterhelfen.

Freundliche Grüße

Konradt G.

Good day

Here is my little help for your project

1.   My Name is Konradt G.

2.   I am 52 years old

3.   I lived in Meschendorf until the age of 17 (1976)

4.   We visited Meschendorf 7 times, and every time we became more aware
that the town has almost totally died out and is abandoned.

    The old houses are left to fall apart.

    As there is almost no one left in Meschendorf, the traditional customs
are being lost as they are not being past on through generations.

5.   This questions is unfortunately not very easy to answer. Honesty and
hard work, a person who dares for a new beginning.

6.   No I do not own a house in Meschendorf, but my families house is
being taken care of by my brother.

Hopefully I could help you with my short answers.

Friendly greetings

Konradt G.

Liebe Frau Klein!

Mein Name ist Harald H,. Ich wohne in Ammerbuch, Jetzt bin 78 Jahre alt.

In der Zeit von Herbst 1961 bis Herbst 1968 war ich Pfarrer in Meschendorf.

Seit ich Meschendorf verlassen habe, war ich sehr oft in dieser kleinen Gemeinde, an der mein Herz hing und noch immer hängt.

Veränderungen, die das heutige Bild Meschendorfs aufweist, sind auf den ersten Blick nicht relevant. Die Häuser sind immer noch so, wie ich sie kannte, wenn auch teilweise renoviert, dank den Bemühungen des britischen Thronfolgers, der sich - ich weiß nicht warum - sehr um siebenbürgische Dörfer kümmert. Aber an einigen Häusern sieht man doch auch, dass die Zeit nicht stille steht und dass der Zahn der Zeit an ihnen nagt. Einige, allerdings wenige, sind auch eingestürzt.

Es leben nur ein paar Sachsen dort, von denen der ehemalige Kirchenvater (aus meiner Zeit) und Kurator der letzten Zeit, eine rühmliche Ausnahme ist. Sein Name ist Martin Werner, besser bekannt unter dem Hofnamen „Knalle-Mitz." Im August 2010 wurde sein hunderter Geburtstag groß gefeiert.

Beeindruckend ist das Engagement einiger junger Meschendorfer für ihr Heimatsdorf. Zum Beispiel Familie Heinz Georg Dörner, Hans Figuli, um nur ein paar Namen zu nennen. Einige haben ihr Haus total renoviert und auf westlichen Standard gebracht. Den Pfarrhof haben sie auf 49 Jahre gemietet und renoviert. Er soll als Gästehaus für Besucher dienen.

Die Kirche ist zum Teil auch renoviert und mit einer Alarmanlage gesichert.

Was definiert einen Siebenbürger Sachsen? Bei dieser Frage muss ich ein wenig in der Vergangenheit greifen. Im 12. Jahrhundert herrschte in ganz Europa das System der Leibeigenschaft. Die Bauern hatten ein schweres Leben. Doch das wissen Sie ja. Das ungarische Königsreich (zu dem auch Siebenbürgen gehörte) wurde von östlichen Völkern immer wieder angegriffen und verwüstet. Der König Geysa und später Bela IV beriefen „Hospites" (Fremde, Gäste) „ad retinendam Coronam" (zum Schutz der Krone) in das Land. Der „Goldene Freibrief" sicherte ihnen Freiheit und Selbstverwaltung. Sie waren nur dem König untertan. Dieser Freibrief hatte, wenn auch nicht mehr in allen Punkten, Gültigkeit, fast bis in das 19. Jahrhundert. Zu meiner Zeit war eigentlich nur noch das Recht der freien Pfarrwahl übrig.

Diese Sonderstellung der Sachsen den andern Ethnien gegenüber, hatte sie stolz gemacht. Bis in unsere Zeit wirkte sich dies aus. Man sagt: „Dummheit und Stolz wachsen auf dem gleichen Holz." Bei den Sachsen hatte das schlimme Folgen. Man sah nur noch auf den Reichtum und suchte den zu mehren. Sehr oft hatte man möglichst nur ein Kind, um durch Heirat mit einem ebensolchen Partner den Reichtum zu mehren. Dass man sich dadurch ins eigene Fleisch schneidet, merkte man erst später - zu spät.

Trotzdem würde ich sagen, ein Siebenbürger ist stolz, aber ohne den Anderen zu diskriminieren. Er ist fleißig und genügsam. Das zeigt die Tatsache, dass beinahe jeder, der nach Deutschland ausgewandert ist, mit seinem Hab und Gut in einem Koffer, nach relativ kurzer Zeit im eigenen Haus lebte.

Ich glaube, dass Sie das alles ja schon längst wissen.

Für Ihre Arbeit wünsche ich Ihnen gutes Vorankommen und auch sonst alles Gute.

Ammerbuch-Poltringen, am 18. Sept.2011

Harald v. H.

My name is Harald H. I live in Ammerbuch, Germany. Now I am 78 years old.
During the time period of autumn 1961 till autumn 1968 I was priest in
Meschendorf.

Since I have left Meschendorf, I have come back to visit this small
community frequently, as my heart still longs for it. Changes that have taken
place in Meschendorf that have changed the present picture of the village
are not relevant on first glance. The houses are still the same as I remember
them, even if some of them have been renovated thanks to the British next in
throne, who - I do not know why- has a great interest in up keeping the Saxon
'Siebenbuergische' villages. Nevertheless, on some houses one can tell that
time has not stood still, and that the tooth of time is biting on them. A
couple houses though, although very few, have even collapsed.

Only a few Saxons remain in Meschendorf. One of the exceptions that
remained, is the past church father (from my time) and curator of the not so
long past. His name is Martin Werner, who is better known under his 'Hofname'
"Knalle-Mitz". In August 2010 there was a large celebration for his 100th
birthday.

Impressive is the engagement of some of the younger Meschendorfer for
their hometown. For example is Heinz Georg Doerner and Hans Figuli to name
a few. Many have totally renovated their home, bringing it up to a more
westernised standard. The 'Pfarrhof' was renovated and rented for 49 years.
It should function as a guesthouse for visitors.

The church has also been party renovated, and is fitted with an alarm.

What defines a 'Siebenbuerger' Saxon? To answer this question I must
reach a bit into the past. In the 12th century the system of selfdom ruled
throughout entire Europe. The farmers had a very difficult life. But I am sure
you are already aware of this. The Hungarian kingdom, (to which also belonged
"Siebenbuergen"), was constantly being attacked and destroyed by eastern
communities. The King Geysa, and later Bela IV appealed for "Hospites"
(foreign guest helpers), "Ad retinendam Coronam" (as protection for the
crown), to aid the country. The "Goldene Freibrief" (Golden Charter), secured
the guest helpers freedom and self-administration. They were only subject to
the King. This 'Golden Charter' was still valid , in most points, into the
19th century. During my time, there was only the right for Freedom of Parish
Election remaining.

This special agreement towards the Saxons compared to other ethnicity had
made the Saxons very proud. This was visible until our time in Meschendorf.
One says 'Stupidity and pride grow on the same wood'. With the Saxons this
had bad consequences. Saxons began to only look at their own wealth, and
tried to multiply this. Very often one possibly only had one child, and then
tried to find an appropriate partner to multiply ones wealth through marriage.
That one cuts oneself in ones own flesh through this method was only realised
later- too late.

Ammeruch-Poltringen, on the 18. Sept. 2011

Harald H.

Montag, 19. September 2011

Hallo Jessica Klein,
es ist schön zu hören, dass Meschendorf nun auch als Vorlage für
wissenschaftliche Arbeiten dient.

Hier meine Antworten:

1.   Name: Hildegard G.
2.   Alter: 41
3.   Bis wann haben Sie in Meschendorf gelebt?: 1990
4.   Wie oft haben Sie Meschendorf seit Ihrer Auswanderung besucht? Was
waren die drei größten Eindrücke? (Veränderungen kulturell, Architektur usw)
:

Ich habe Meschendorf seither nur 3 Mal besucht. Zuletzt 1997. Emotional
war jeder Besuch. Die Veränderungen in der Bevölkerung als auch in der
Architektur waren dramatisch. Häuser waren eingefallen, man konnte kein
Bestreben nach Aufbau erkennen. Inzwischen soll das wohl anders sein.

5.   Sie sind per Geburt Siebenbürger Sachse. Was definiert einen
Siebenbürger Sachsen? (Falls Sie in Deutschland geboren sind: welche
Antwort würden Sie geben?). Ich bin von Geburt Siebenbürger Sachse. Großes
Durchhaltevermögen, ein Sachse ist zäh und treu, einfach, zuverlässig. Fühlt
sich am wohlsten unter Seinesgleichen (die Generationen vor uns).

6.   Gehört ihnen noch ein Haus/Grundstueck in Meschendorf? NEIN

7.   Schliesslich: Wenn sie noch weitere Information über Meschendorfer
Architektur, Traditionen und Tägliches Leben ergänzenm wollen – bitte
schildern Sie es hier. Ich bin für jede Auskunft dankbar..

   Zu diesem Punkt kann ich nur Auskunft geben über die Jahre bis 1990: Häuser
sind überraschend funktionell gebaut. Mehrere Generationen haben unter
einem Dach gewohnt. Das Dorfleben war von der Landwirtschaft geprägt. Alle
Familienmitglieder haben mitgearbeitet. An Sonn- und Feiertagen wurde in
der Dorf- oder Familiengemeinschaft gefeiert. Die Dorfjugend hat die freien
Abende und Feiern zusammen verbracht. Jeder kannte Jeden. Jeder hat Jeden
gegrüßt.

Kirche und Schule/Kindergarten haben den Mittelpunkt gebildet. Eine große
Integration in die Gemeinschaft mit den im Dorf Lebenden Rumänen hat nicht
stattgefunden. Dias Dorf war in Nachbarschaften organisiert.

Es wäre schön wenn Sie uns an den Ergebnissen Ihrer Arbeit beteiligen
könnten. Ich wünsche Ihnen viel Erfolg!

Hildegard G.

146

Monday 19th September 2011

Dear Jessica Klein,

It is nice to hear that now Meschendorf has become of interest for a research paper.

1. Name: Hildegard G.
2. Age: 41
3. Until what date did you live in Meschendorf? 1990

4. How often did you visit Meschendorf since you emigrated? What were the three greatest impressions? (changes culturally, architecturally etc):

I have only visited Meschendorf three times. The last time was in 1997. Every visit was very emotional. The changes in the community, as also in the architecture were dramatic. Houses had callapsed and you could not see any effort to maintain the community after re-building. Nowerdays it is meant to be different.

5. Are you a 'Siebenbuerger' Saxon by birth? What defines a 'Siebenbuerger' Saxon?

I am a 'Siebenbuerger' Saxon by birth. A Saxon has great stamina, is tough and loyal, he is also very trustworthy. Feels mostly at home under his/her own people (the generation before us).

6. Do you still own a house or property in Meschendorf? No

7. Finally: If you have any further information you could add regarding Meschendorf architecture, tradition, and daily life I would be grateful for any information.

To this point I can only give information up to the year 1990: Houses are surprisingly built very functional. Multiple generations lived together under one roof. The village life was taken over through agricultural activities. All family members worked together. On Sundays or holidays there were always celebrations in the village Tanzplatz or community hall. The youngsters always spent their free evenings and holidays together. Everyone knew everyone and everyone greeted everyone.

The church and the school/kindergarten created the centre point of the village. A large integration with the Romanians living in the village never took place. The village was organised in 'Nachbarschaften'.

It would be nice if you could keep me up to date with the process and result of your project. I wish you great success.

Hildegard G.

29.9.11

Hallo Jessica,

ich bin leider etwas spät dran mit dem Fragebogen..... aber dennoch möchte
ich ihn Dir soweit es mir möglich ist, beantworten.
Ich hoffe Du hattest bisher einige Rückmeldungen und hoffentlich brauchbare?

Kennst Du unser "Meschendorfer Nachbarschaftszeichen"? Hat Dir von dem schon
Jemand was erzählt? Das erscheint einmal im Jahr, ist sozusagen eine Art
Zeitung von der HOG Meschendorf e.V. (HOG=Heimatsortsgemeinschaft) - dort
werden über das ganze Jahr Berichte, Beiträge, Fotos etc. gesammelt und wird
dann einmal im Jahr als gebundene Zeitschrift veröffentlicht.

1.   Name: Sieglinde K,
2.   Alter: 41 (geb. 28.02.1970)

3.   Bis wann haben Sie in Meschendorf gelebt? bis 1982

4.   Wie oft haben Sie Meschendorf seit Ihrer Auswanderung besucht? Was
waren die drei größten Eindrücke? (Veränderungen kulturell, Architektur
usw) bis ca. 1990 jährlich, seit 1990 sehr sporadisch, alle paar Jahre. Bis
1990 waren Verwandte, Freunde und Bekannte in Meschendorf und bis dahin fast
unverändertes Dorfleben wie ich es in meiner Kindheit dort erlebt hatte, nach
1990 (Grenzfall) also nach der Auswanderung der Meschendorfer Sachsen, Tod
von Oma etc. war Meschendorf sehr einsam und verlassen - totale Veränderung
- nach einigen Jahren massiver Verfall der unbewohnten Häuser, was einen sehr
traurigen Eindruck in mir erweckte. Nachdem wieder einige Jahre vergangen
waren, wurden wieder einige Häuser renoviert, was aber mein gewohntes
Dorfbild total veränderte und Meschendorf mir dann doch sehr fremd vorkam.

5.   Sie sind per Geburt Siebenbürger Sachse. Was definiert einen
Siebenbürger Sachsen? (Falls Sie in Deutschland geboren sind: welche
Antwort würden Sie geben?) ja gebürtig. Was definiert ihn? Gastfreundlich,
zuverlässig, freundlich, fleißig.

6.   Gehört ihnen noch ein Haus/Grundstueck in Meschendorf? mir nicht,
aber meinen Eltern (Martin und Frieda Klein)

Wünsche Dir eine gute Zeit!

Dear Jessica

I am a bit late with answering the questions, never the less I wish to answer
them as much as is possible.

I hope that you already managed to get a lot of replies, and useful ones?

Do you know our "Meschendorfer Nachbarschafszeichen"? Did anyone already tell
you about this? It appears to be released once a yaer and is a type of News-
paper from the HOG Meschendorf e.V. (HOG + Heimatsortsgemeinschaft) - over
the year reports, writings, photos etc are collected and released once a year
as a bound magazine.

1.   Sieglinde K.
2.   2 41 (Born 28.02.1970)
3.   until 1982
4.   until around 1990 annually, since 1990 very sporadically every couple
of years. Until 1990 there were still remaining relatives, friends and ac-
quaintance in Meschendorf, in addition to an unchanged village life just how
I experienced it during my childhood. After 1990 (the fall of curtain wall)
So after the emigration of the Meschendorfer Saxons, the death of my grandma
etc. Meschendorf became very lonely and abandoned - total change- after a
couple years the abandoned houses collapsed, which awakes a very sad feeling
in me. After a couple more years passed, many of the remaining houses were
renovated, which though changed my picture/vision of the village, and as a
result made Meschendorf appear foreign to me.

5.   Yes I was born there. What defines a Saxon? Guest-friendly, reliable,
friendly and hardworking.

6.   I don't own a house/property, but my parents do (Martin and Frieda
Klein)

I wish you a good time

Lots of wishes Sieglinde

16/9/11

1.   Name: Markus K.

2.   Alter: 17

3.   Bis wann haben Sie in Meschendorf gelebt? gar nicht

4.   Wie oft haben Sie Meschendorf seit Ihrer Auswanderung besucht? Was
waren die drei größten Eindrücke? (Veränderungen kulturell, Architektur usw)

ich habe meschendorf vier mal besucht. zu den 3 größten eindrücken gehörten
das leben im allgemeinen dort, d.h. die art und weise wie ich mir beispiels-
weise etwas zu essen koche oder ich mich wasche.

außerdem fand ich es damals sehr intressant mit dem pferdewagen zu fahren.
am eindrucksvollsten fand ich jedoch den maigraben und steinberg. dort zeigt
sich vorallem die unberührte natur rumäniens.

5.   Sie sind per Geburt Siebenbürger Sachse. Was definiert einen Siebenbürger Sachsen? (Falls Sie in Deutschland geboren sind: welche Antwort würden
Sie geben?)

ich glaube ein sachse wird durch eine art einheitsgefühl für einander definiert.

6.   Gehört ihnen noch ein Haus/Grundstueck in Meschendorf?

meiner oma, meiner mutter und meinem opa gehören verschiedene grundstücke mit
verschiedenen häusern, u.a. in neudorf und meschendorf

7.   Schliesslich: Wenn sie noch weitere Information über Meschendorfer Architektur, Traditionen und Tägliches Leben ergänzenm wollen - bitte schildern
Sie es hier. Ich bin für jede Auskunft dankbar..

tut mir leid, ich hab nichts hinzu zufügen

1. Name : Markus K.

2. Age: 17

3. Until which date did you live in Meschendorf?
never

4. Since you emigrated from Meschendorf, how often have you visited Meschendorf? What were your three greatest impressions? (changes in culture, architecture etc)

I have been in Meschendorf 4 times. The 3 greatest impessions: The life style
in the village, for example simple things like the way you cook, or wash
yourself.

I also found it very intersting to ride in the horse wagon, The most impressive natural feature there tho was teh Maigraben am Steinberg where you can
see the untouched nature of Romania.

5. Are you Siebenbürger Saxon from birth? What defines a Siebenbürger Saxon?
(incase you were born in Germany are you Saxon or German?)

6. Do you still own property in Meschendorf?

7. If you have any further information on Meschendorf please let me know. I
am grateful for any information and thoughts.

Drawings

Meschendorf Sieberbürger Saxons

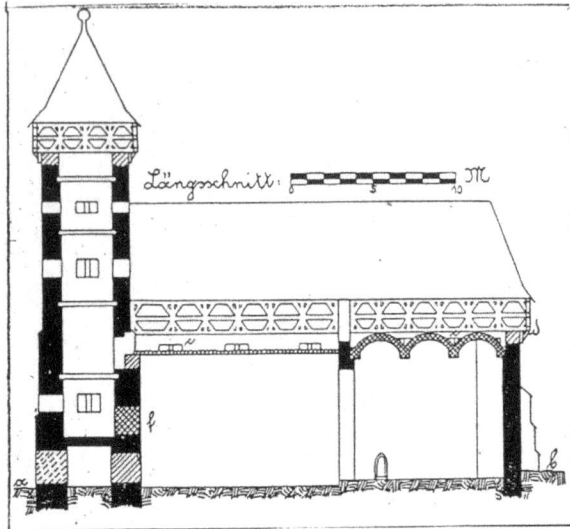

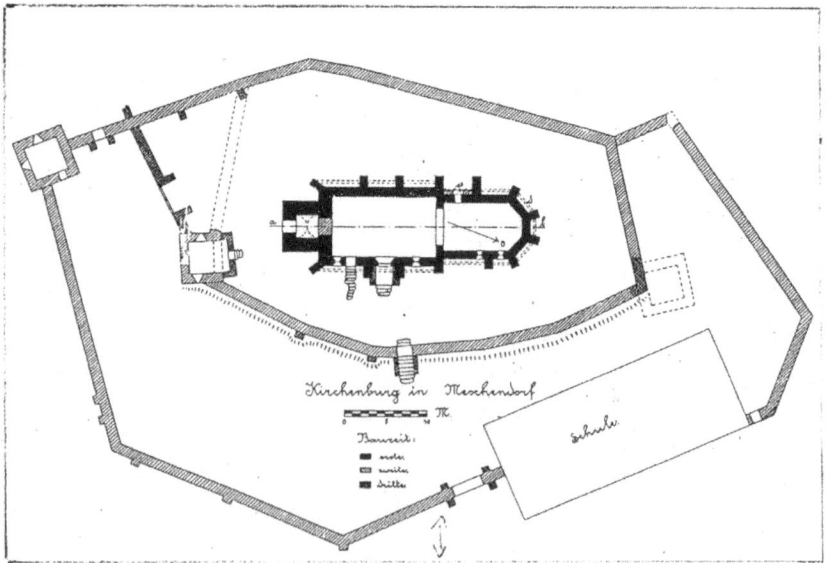

Plan of Fortified Church (1930), Walter Horwath

(Toepfer, Friedrich. P. 230)

154

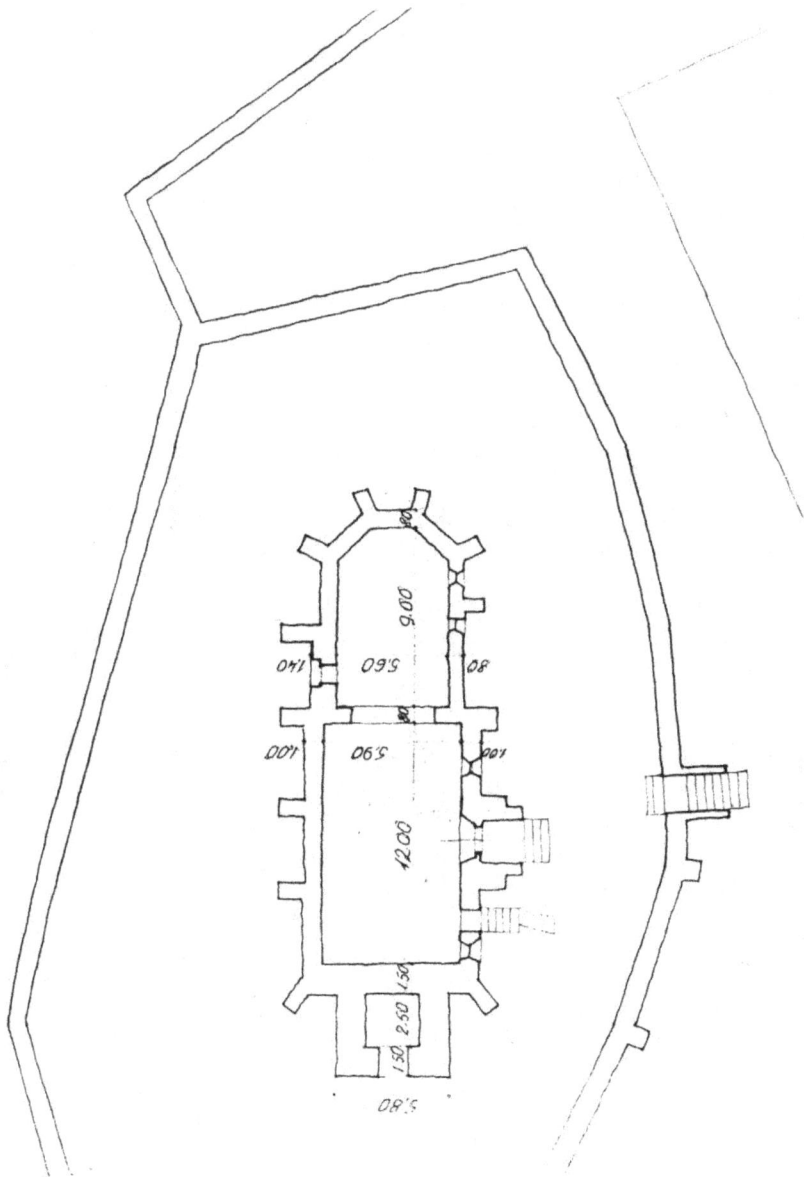

Measurements of Church (1967) Architect: Ing. Krasser

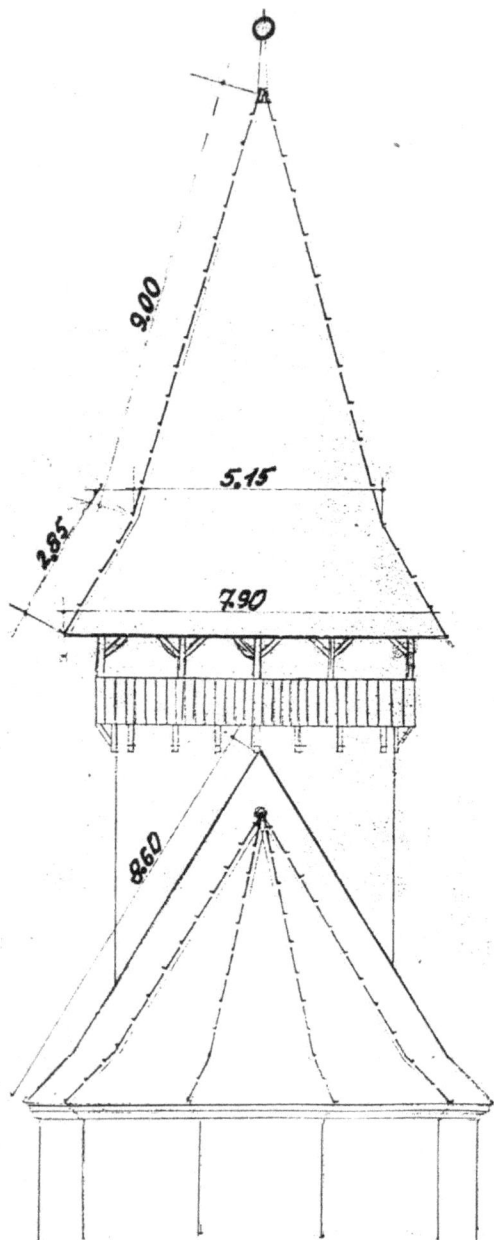

Measurements of Church Tower (1967), Architect: Ing. Krasser

(Toepfer, Friedrich. P. 232)

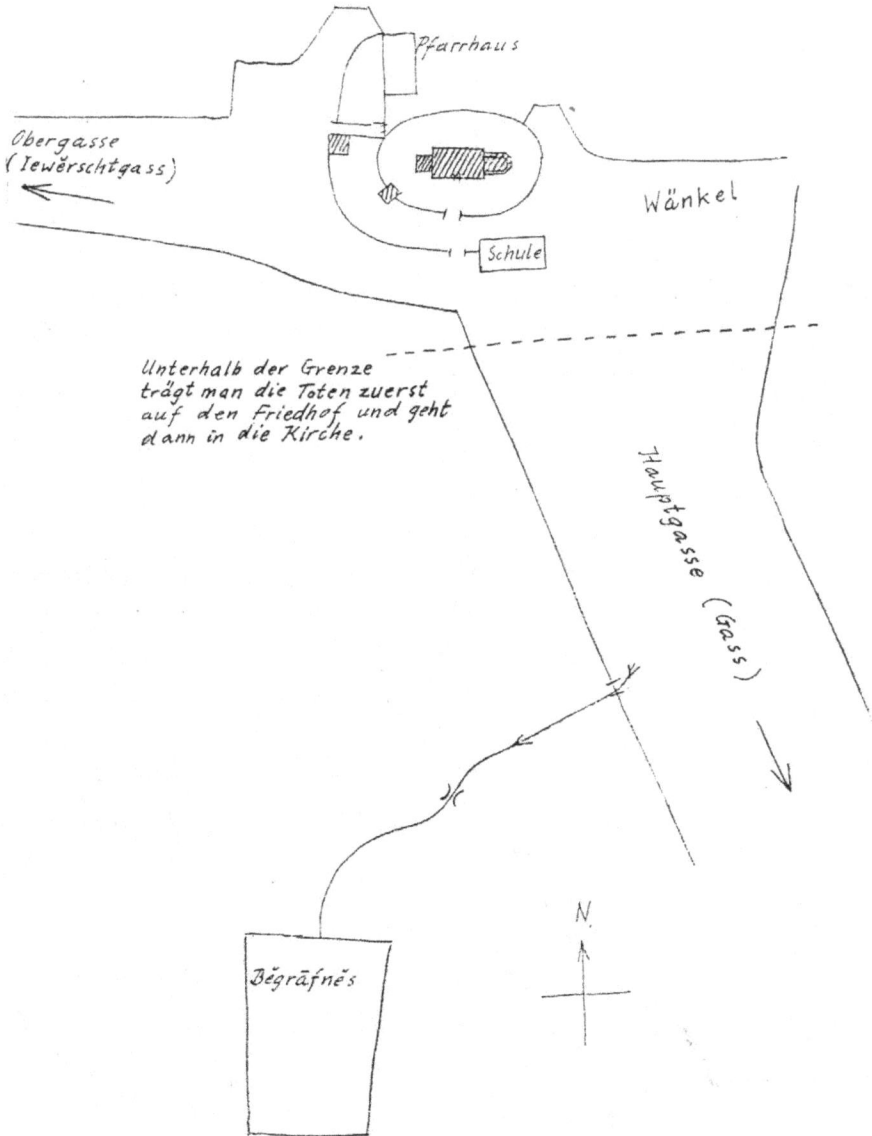

Lageplan (ungefähr)

Pfarrhaus

Obergasse (Iewërschtgass)

Wänkel

Schule

Unterhalb der Grenze trägt man die Toten zuerst auf den Friedhof und geht dann in die Kirche.

Hauptgasse (Gass)

N.

Begräfnes

(Toepfer, Friedrich. P. 242)

Relationship of Lutheran Church to Graveyard (1961) . Gerhardt Binder

Thank you to Martin, Friedchen
and Helmuth Klein who invited me
to their home in Meschendorf,
Transylvania and have aided me
throughout my research.

Also thank you to my father
Roland Klein who accompanied me
on this journey.